S0-BBZ-263

HURON COUNTY LIBRARY

3 6492 0049344 1

DATE DUE

JUL 2 4 2004			
MAY 2 0 2005			

951.9304092 KimCh -B

Breen, M.
Kim Jong-Il.

PRICE: $35.99 (3559/se)

More Praise for *Kim Jong-il: North Korea's Dear Leader*

North Korea is the final frontier, the last hold out of a personality-based dictatorship regime that has the power to destabilize Asia's drive to prosperity. Ignore North Korea and you'll ignore the biggest risk to Asia's prosperity. This book provides unique insights into the internal dynamics of the Dark Kingdom and no one who commits capital to Asia can afford to miss it.

Jesper Koll
Chief Japan Analyst, Merrill Lynch Japan

As the world turns its attention to the hermit kingdom of north Asia, there is no better introduction than Michael Breen's book, which combines the freshness of journalism with the insights of long experience. Here we find every aspect of North Korea and its "Glorious Sun of the 21st Century" Kim Jong-il - the fanaticism, the farce, and most of all the tragedy. History demands that this place and this man be recorded. Breen's book will be widely read.

Bruce Gilley
Former contributing editor, *Far Eastern Economic Review*
Co-author of *China's New Rulers: The Secret Files*

This book could not be more timely. At a time when the Korean peninsula faces a renewed crisis, an understanding of the North Korean mindset is crucial in dealing with the situation. Michael Breen provides a rich and illustrative introduction of Kim Jong-il as an individual and as the North's leader. This book should be on the reading list of anybody interested in Korean affairs.

⁃ Francis Schortgen
Business Consultant and Analyst (South Korea)

Defying predictions of early collapse, the DPRK has endured. The international community cannot ignore North Korea and wish the regime would go away when international security and humanitarian crises are lurking within. Michael Breen provides an in-depth look into Kim Jong-il and the domestic system that both created and constrains him, which is essential for understanding North Korean behavior and intentions. I highly recommend this book to anyone interested in North Korean affairs.

Daniel A. Pinkston
Senior Research Associate, Center for Nonproliferation Studies
Monterey Institute of International Studies

KIM JONG-IL
North Korea's Dear Leader

KIM JONG-IL
North Korea's Dear Leader

Michael Breen

John Wiley & Sons (Asia) Pte Ltd

Copyright © 2004 John Wiley & Sons (Asia) Pte Ltd
Published in 2004 by John Wiley & Sons (Asia) Pte Ltd
2 Clementi Loop, #02-01, Singapore 129809

All rights reserved.

No part of this publication may be reproduced, stored in a retrieval system or transmitted in any form or by any means, electronic, mechanical, photocopying, recording, scanning or otherwise, except as expressly permitted by law, without either the prior written permission of the Publisher, or authorization through payment of the appropriate photocopy fee to the Copyright Clearance Center. Requests for permission should be addressed to the Publisher, John Wiley & Sons (Asia) Pte Ltd, 2 Clementi Loop, #02-01, Singapore 129809, tel: 65-64632400, fax: 65-64646912, e-mail: enquiry@wiley.com.sg.

This publication is designed to provide accurate and authoritative information in regard to the subject matter covered. It is sold with the understanding that the publisher is not engaged in rendering professional services. If professional advice or other expert assistance is required, the services of a competent professional person should be sought.

Other Wiley Editorial Offices

John Wiley & Sons, Inc., 111 River Street, Hoboken, NJ 07030, USA
John Wiley & Sons Ltd, The Atrium, Southern Gate, Chichester PO19 8SQ, England
John Wiley & Sons (Canada) Ltd, 22 Worcester Road, Rexdale, Ontario M9W 1L1, Canada
John Wiley & Sons Australia Ltd, 33 Park Road (PO Box 1226), Milton, Queensland 4064, Australia
Wiley-VCH, Pappelallee 3, 69469 Weinheim, Germany

Library of Congress Cataloging-in-Publication Data
0-470-82131-0

Typeset in 11/15 points, New Baskerville by Linographic Services Pte Ltd
Printed in Singapore by Saik Wah Press Pte Ltd
10 9 8 7 6 5 4 3 2 1

Contents

CHINA

Rajin

Chongjin

RUSSIAN FED.

NORTH
KOREA

Dandong

Sinuiju

Hamhung

Yongbyun

Wonsan

Nampo

PYONGYANG

East Sea
(Sea of Japan)

Haeju

Kaesong

Incheon

SEOUL

SOUTH
KOREA

Yellow
Sea

Daegu

Gwangju

Busan

JAPAN

0   100 km

0   100 miles

Jeju
Island

Preface

In the summer of 2002, the United States concluded that North Korea was running a secret nuclear weapons program in violation of international obligations. Tensions worsened when, in early 2003, North Korea became the first country to withdraw from the international Nuclear Nonproliferation Treaty.

The United States viewed this step with extreme alarm. During their long alliance, the United States and South Korea have committed soldiers to a combined force in South Korea to deter aggression from the communist North. Things had been looking up since 2000, when the South's Kim Dae-jung and the North's Kim Jong-il held a historic first-ever summit. Later the same year, US Secretary of State Madeleine Albright had visited Pyongyang. Hopes for reconciliation had been higher than ever before.

But the latest revelations turned the clock back. At the time, American troops had ousted the regime in Afghanistan and would soon be engaged in Iraq. Instead of looking at North Korea through a Cold War lens as a "communist threat," Washington was viewing it as a potential ally of rogue states and terrorist groups. The War on Terror had come to Cold War Korea, bringing with it the likelihood of conflict.

Koreans are familiar with such highs and lows. Their country has long been a land of drama and extremes.

Its rift into pro-Soviet North and pro-American South in 1945 was the most extreme among divided nations in modern history. Three million Koreans died when the two sides went to war. In the South, you will find Asia's most fervent Christians. The North has produced a communist personality cult that was — and remains — more fanatic even than those of Mao or Stalin.

Entering the twenty-first century, the North is exhausted by food shortages and economic decline, while the South is the world's twelfth largest economy.

For all its bizarre fanaticism, North Korea has not been of much interest to the international community. Since the 1950–53 Korean War, it has only occasionally poked out of its self-imposed isolation and grabbed our attention. Each time has been for some negative reason — assassination attempts on South Korean presidents; arrests of its diplomats for drug smuggling; training of terrorists; the seizure in 1968 of the USS Pueblo, a spy ship, and its crew; the 1976 axe murders of two American officers in the demilitarized zone (DMZ); the death of Kim Il-sung in 1994; famine; defectors. The only positive story I remember was when North Korea's soccer players stunned the world by beating Italy to get into the quarter-finals of the 1966 World Cup. The people of the English city of Middlesborough, where they played their matches, became instant North Korea fans. The Korean technique was to run all over the place through the entire match, a style that later became known as "total football."

In recent years, North Korea has leapt back into the news. Indeed, in the early 2000s, even before the nuclear flare-up, it took international center stage. This arrival began as an afterthought. When the White House was preparing President George W. Bush's 2002 State of the Union address, North Korea got slipped into the now-famous "Axis of Evil," alongside Iraq and Iran, apparently at the last minute and very possibly for reasons of style and political correctness, not policy.[1] Somehow an axis of just two Muslim states didn't seem complete.

A lot of people winced when they heard this, although not because they didn't think North Korea was evil. They knew it had no connection to Islamic terrorism — certainly not enough to warrant "Axis of Evil" membership — and thought that this new label would ruin efforts underway in South Korea to coax the North out of its hopeless isolation. The effect was to put what had always been a minor league rogue state high up there on the US presidential agenda.

My own interest in Kim Jong-il and North Korea goes back to 1982, when I moved from New York to Seoul to work as a freelance journalist. At that time, Kim Jong-il's father, Kim Il-sung, was in power. We in South Korea feared him.

In the late 1980s, North Korea opened up to western tourists and so I decided to take a look. I dropped in beforehand on an ambassador from a friendly country for what turned out to be a spot of informal spy training.

"They won't tell you anything," he said. (Or they'll lie, I later discovered. My first guide would claim that crime did not exist in North Korea.) "You'll have to figure things out from what you see."

Seek truth from the window. The first impressions — oxen in the fields, an absence of commerce, wacky political slogans, children marching to school singing revolutionary songs, decrepit industry — made me wonder why we were afraid of this sad country. Count the wires between telegraph poles, the ambassador had advised (I forget what the calculation was for, but a lot of poles had just one). "See what kind of rolling stock is in the train stations."

So I did this, and discovered my inner Sherlock Holmes.

"Why are there so many broken bottles at the capping machine?" I wondered, Watson-like, with a colleague when we were taken to a soft drinks plant outside the capital, Pyongyang. "These bottles aren't sitting straight on the line," he offered and took one off to examine it. "That's because there are bubbles sticking out of the bottom. They're at an angle and, when the machine rams the cap down, it cracks them." You know you've come alive when even the glass industry can fascinate you.

It's but a small step from such observations to solutions — like, how's about upgrading bottle-making technology? — and soon your foreign visitor starts to feel like an expert in nation-building. Thus outsiders become hooked on North Korea. All, even those who appear to be supporters, know North Korea is in the grip of a nauseating dictatorship, but from a position of safety as foreigners, they cherish their association with it because of how it makes them feel about themselves.

Thus engaged, you find you can develop sympathy for the people even though they are figuratively blindfolding and spinning you round. Once, in the mid-1990s, when the foreign press was reporting rice shortages, the Koryo Hotel in Pyongyang was serving two bowls of rice with each meal, proving, I thought, that the reports were wrong. "No, it confirms them," a South Korean friend later explained before I went into print with my discovery. "They know you won't eat it all. They're taking the leftovers home."

Welcome to North Korea, a mysterious state with a remarkable ability to run rings around the outside world, a country where information and mobility are so restricted that citizens don't know what's going on outside and no-one knows what's going on inside. North Korea for years has been what one US diplomat once dubbed an "intelligence black hole."

We believe, but are not sure, that as many as three million people may have died of famine, and that hundreds of thousands more have fled to China, where they live secretly and in fear of deportation and punishment.[2] How is a humanitarian crisis on this scale possible in the twenty-first century in the center of booming Northeast Asia?

The answer lies with the one fat man in the whole country, Kim Jong-il. The aim of this book is to introduce him, to tell his story as far as possible, and to figure how he reconciles the fact that his citizens can be sent to the gulag for reading *Le Monde* with his personal preference for a good French wine.

In doing this, we should also explore the curious question of how he manages to hold on to power. Why have the North Koreans not dumped their brand of Communism onto the ash heap of history, especially as a better way to be Korean, practically-speaking, is offered by the prosperous, free South? Does it retain some nationalistic appeal, or is the regime so fearfully repressive that the people are unable to reject it? Alternatively, is the answer simply that North Koreans love their leader?

Above all, we need to examine why Kim's shriveling odiocracy of a regime is able to scare the civilized world with its weapons of mass destruction. This last question exposes us. For as much as the humanitarian crisis and human rights abuses of North Korea should concern us, it is its apparent willingness to wage awful war that makes us most anxious for ourselves.

Kim Jong-il's nuclear program puts North Korea on a collision course with the United States and its allies. Europe, Russia, China, South Korea, and Japan all agree that North Korea + Nukes is a disastrous formula, even if they disagree on how to deal with it. As hard as it is to believe from the sophisticated malls of Seoul, Tokyo, and Beijing, this situation is very likely to end in warfare. And the best argument for believing this is the realization that the post-September 11 government in the United States and the isolated government in Pyongyang live on different planets, and have no clue what the other wants. Suddenly, knowing North Korea is no longer a specialist interest. The world has a stake in understanding what it can about this man and his country.

This knowledge needs to be sensible if it is to inform strategies for dealing with Kim. One consequence of his nuclear fame is that Kim Jong-il has become famously demonized. In one week in January 2003, he made the cover of *The Economist*, *Time* and *Newsweek*, in the latter case as "Dr Evil." While understandable — for the world fears him — demonizing Kim complicates efforts to work out how to deal with him, and has the effect of feeding on itself.

We may arrive at straightforward conclusions (for example, Kim has got to go — or not, because a post-Kim regime may be even worse), but we must do so with sound logic. In other words, while being neutral in the face of bad leadership is unacceptable, being objective is essential in assessing it. I say this because another thing my friendly ambassador — who was Australian, if you're bursting to know — said on the eve of that first trip, was, "Can you be objective?" He doubted it because by then I'd lived for seven years in anti-communist South Korea, which portrayed Kim Jong-il as a mad Caligula. (An irony now, of course, is that while the world thinks he has horns, the South Koreans have changed their minds and are now taking the approach that he is a man with whom they can do business.)

In putting these thoughts together, I have relied heavily on a number of people whom I consider to be more expert than myself. Some are authors, whose works I have listed in the bibliography. Others are officials, frequent visitors to North Korea, or defectors, who for personal or professional reasons asked to remain anonymous. Those I can name are: Marceli Burdelski, Jack Burton, Brent Choi, Barbara Demick, Kwak Dae-jung, John Larkin, Donald Macintyre, Tim Peters, Sohn Kwang-joo, Jay Solomon, Norbert Vollertsen, Andrew Ward, and Roland Wein. For additional help, I am grateful to Chi Jungnam, Ken Kaliher, Kim Mi-young, Kim Yooseung, and Ryoo Hwa-joo.

I would like to make special mention of Aidan Foster-Carter, whose copy I had the good fortune of editing some years back when we produced a monthly called *North Korea Report*. He taught me how to laugh at dictatorship.

I would like to thank Nick Wallwork and Janis Soo at John Wiley. The original suggestion for this book came from Nick, when I approached him with a different project. I'm grateful that he had me change course.

I owe huge thanks to my wife, Jennifer Nicholson-Breen, for enduring five months of that particular type of loneliness — your spouse is there but has his mind on something else — while I was writing, and then for applying her professional editing skills to the manuscript. And I should also mention my children, Sasha, Jonnie and Avielle, who live at the other side of the world, and whose summer vacation in 2003 was postponed so that I could complete this project.

Finally, I have dedicated this book to Han Jin-duk, whose brief story appears at the end of Chapter 9. I do not know her, and do not even know if she is dead or alive, but I consider her to be representative of millions of North Koreans whose lives can never be given back.

A Note on Korean Spelling and Names

Korean doesn't lend itself to perfect rendition into English spelling, which is why you will see, in the bibliography for example, Kim Il-sung spelled *Kim Il-song* in some cases with a little symbol above the 'o'. (This, incidentally, is how the CIA does it). In some other books, you will see Jong-il spelt *Chong*-il. But I'm going with the familiar.

Korean names consist of a one-syllable surname first (two in rare cases), followed by a personal name of either one or two syllables. Kim Il-sung is therefore Mr. Kim, not Mr. Sung. There is no fixed style, but I am hyphenating the two-syllable names with the second one lower case, i.e. Kim Jong-il as opposed to Kim Jong-Il or Kim Jong Il. The only exception is in the bibliography. Some Koreans invert their names for simplicity. Again, the only examples here are in the bibliography or in quoted excerpts.

There are only 270 surnames to go around the 75 million or so Koreans in the world, and many of those are obscure. It was only about 100 years ago that all Koreans were required to have a full name, and they naturally tended to choose ones associated with the upper classes. Hence the fact that around one quarter today are named Kim, and another quarter Lee, Park, Choi or Chung. To assist the reader, I have provided a cast of characters who appear in the book.

Korean Names

The following is a list of Koreans who appear in the book and their connection to Kim Jong-il:

Ahn Jong-ho, deputy chief of staff, said to have masterminded a coup attempt in 1992

Ahn Myong-chol, prison guard, defected to South Korea

Chang Myun, South Korean prime minister in 1960

Chang Song-taek, brother-in-law

Choe Hyon, Kim Il-sung's guerrilla colleague

Choe Kwang, Kim Il-sung's guerrilla colleague

Choi Dong-chul, prison guard, defected to South Korea

Choi Eun-hee, South Korean actress kidnapped by Kim Jong-il

Choi Sul-rung, prisoner

Choi Young-hwan, torture victim

Chong Kyong-hui, North Korean woman introduced to Choi Eun-hee by Kim Jong-il

Chun Doo-hwan, South Korean ruler 1980–88

Chung Ju-yung, North Korean-born founder of the South Korean Hyundai Group

Chung Mong-hun, Hyundai executive and son of Chung Ju-yung

Han Byol, name given to Kim Il-sung by his comrades, meaning "One Star"

Han Jin-duk, prisoner

Han Seong-hee, alleged to be Kim Il-sung's first wife

Han Yong-suk, assumed name of Han Seong-hee

Ho Dam, North Korean foreign minister

Hong Il-chon, mistress

Hwang Jang-yop, creator of *Juche* philosophy who defected to South Korea

Kang Chol-hwan, prisoner, defected to South Korea

Kang Myong-do, defector and son of premier Kang Song-san

Kang Pan-seok, paternal grandmother

Kim Chong-tae, founder in South Korea of the Revolutionary Party for Reunification

Kim Bung-ok, prisoner

Kim Chun-ho, interrogated Lee Soon-ok

Kim Chun-hwa, prisoner

Kim Dae-jung, South Korean president 1998–2003

Kim Dok-hong, defected to South Korea with Hwang Jang-yop

Kim Hak-nam, interrogated Lee Soon-ok

Kim Hyeong-jik, paternal grandfather

Kim Hye-kyong, daughter

Kim Hye-sun, alias given to Japanese police by Han Seong-hee

Kim Hyong-wook, head of South Korean CIA under Park Chung-hee

Kim Il, guerrilla veteran

Kim Il-sung, father and founding president of North Korea

Kim Jong-chul, son

Kim Jong-il

Kim Jong-nam, son

Kim Jong-suk, mother

Kim Jung-eun, Korean-American documentary film-maker

Kim Jung-ok, prisoner

Kim Kyung-hee, sister

Kim Kyung-jin, half-sister

Kim Man-il, brother

Kim Ok-sun, wife of Choe Kwang

Kim Pyong-il, half-brother

Kim Shin-jo, North Korean commando captured in Seoul in 1968

Kim Shin-ok, prisoner

Kim Shin-sook, niece of Kim Il-sung who managed Jong-il's college education

Kim Sol-song, daughter

Kim Song-ae, stepmother

Kim Song-ju, Kim Il-sung's original name

Kim Woong-kil, torture victim

Kim Yong-il, half-brother

Kim Yong-ju, uncle

Kim Yong-soon, party secretary

Kim Yong-chul, defector who had worked in the drug trade

Kim Young-sam, South Korean president 1993–98

Kim Young-hee, prisoner

Kim Young-sook, official wife picked by his father

Kim Young-sook, prisoner

Ko Young-hee, mother of Jong-il's likely heir, Kim Jong-chul

Kojong, last king of Korea

Lee Han-yong, nephew

Lee Hoi-chang, opposition presidential candidate in South Korea's 2002 election

Lee Kun-hu, South Korean psychologist

Lee Min, friend of his mother

Lee Myong-jae, official who got Jong-il's permission to execute his wife

Lee Ok-dan, prisoner

Lee Soon-ok, prisoner, defected to South Korea

Lee Yun-chel, torture victim

Lim Chun-chu, intellectual who first proposed Kim Jong-il as the successor

Le Ul-sol, Kim Il-sung's aide-de-camp

Moon Myong-ja, Korean-American journalist

Moon Sun-myung, North Korea-born founder of the Unification Church

O Jin-u, guerrilla veteran

Park Chung-hee, South Korean ruler 1961–79

Park Seung-jin, prisoner and member of North Korea's World Cup soccer team in 1966

Rhee Syngman, South Korean president 1948–60

Roh Moo-hyun, South Korean president since 2003

Roh Tae-woo, head of Seoul Olympic Organizing Committee, South Korean president 1988–93

Shin Sang-ok, South Korean movie director kidnapped by Kim Jong-il

Suh Young-sun, prisoner

Sung Hae-rang, sister-in-law

Sung Hae-rim, common-law wife

Yi Jae-dok, wet nurse

Dark Country

I f you could scan Northeast Asia from space at night — which
the United States does, for obvious reasons — you'd pick up
something odd. Amid the bright lights of China, South
Korea, and Japan lies a pool of darkness: North Korea.

The black patch is home to 23 million people whose total
available energy wouldn't light up a single town across the border
in South Korea. Theirs is no Pacific idyll of sandy beaches and
grass skirts that doesn't need electricity. The ocean's giant fists
have squeezed the Korean peninsula into mountain ridges,
making four-fifths of it uninhabitable. It steams in mid-summer
and goes 20-below in winter. You need air conditioning and
central heating, as well as lights, to function. You also need fuel.
The Democratic People's Republic of Korea, as it's called, is an
industrialized state, mechanized and heavy-industry friendly in
the communist fashion, where in better days heroines in hard
hats posed for pictures with their tractors. It's also slap in the
middle of the world's booming region-that-never-sleeps, a three-
hour flight from 40 cities with populations of over one million.
It should be humming, but much of its population is in rags,
literally living off grass, and struggling in heartbreaking misery.

Why?

For answers, you look to spots of lesser gloom. Like, say, the
energy-guzzling Kumsusan Memorial Palace on the edge of the

1

capital, Pyongyang. This was once the country's White House, where the Republic's founding leader, Kim Il-sung, lived and worked and received visitors. After his death in 1994 his son and heir, Kim Jong-il, who had other quarters in the capital, had the imposing granite edifice turned into a mausoleum. Elaborate equipment has been installed in this pyramid to sanitize visitors, as if they were entering a semiconductor plant. Visitors say there's a section of revolving brushes that clean the soles of your shoes, a half-mile of moving walkways, X-ray machines and sections where the dirt is air-blasted off your clothes. A marble corridor spits you out into a chamber featuring a white statue of the deceased Mr Kim, illuminated from behind by pink lights. Finally you reach a vast, darkened hall, filled with somber music. Lit up in the center is a black bier upon which Kim Il-sung lies under glass in a black suit, brought to near-life by Russian embalmers.

The whole job, embalming and decoration, is believed to have cost US$100 million, a chunky amount for a country with an annual trade of a couple of billion, but what price devotion?[1] Ordinary North Koreans often burst into tears when they catch sight of Mr Kim and, one assumes, wouldn't begrudge the cash, which anyway is too vast for them to conceive of.

In life, the senior Mr Kim was long referred to as the *weedaehan suryong-nim*, or "Great Leader." In his time, he was also variously referred to as "the Peerless Patriot," "the Ever-Victorious Iron-Willed Brilliant Commander," "the Sun of the Nation," "the Sun of Mankind," "the Red Sun of the Oppressed People," and more. He was posthumously given the title, "Eternal President."

"He is the most famous man in the world," a sincere young student told me in Pyongyang once. Obviously not a shy fellow, Kim senior welcomed statues of himself in town squares, the biggest being a 20-meter bronze job painted in gold and unveiled on his sixtieth birthday in 1972. It overlooks Kim Il-sung Square, a short jeep ride from Kim Il-sung University and Kim Il-sung Stadium. In the streets and fields, every adult citizen wears a badge bearing his likeness and, when they get home after a hard day's listening to songs about him, they can gaze at the obligatory pictures of him and Jong-il that hang in every home. There's a revolutionary museum all about how he built the "workers' paradise." The country's opera, theater, art, literature, and music are all about him. "I put forward the proposal of a 50-to-50 ratio between the creative works of the socialist construction and the revolutionary struggle," he said in a guidance speech to writers.[2] In other words, half of culture is to be about my activities as an independence fighter against Japan and half about my nation-building. The Red Sun of the Oppressed People further "put forward the proposal" that literature should not be about the life stories of comrades who are still living and might become popular, but rather about comrades who sacrificed their lives — for him. So far, no North Korean has been short-listed for the Nobel Prize for Literature.

A tower commemorating his version of Communism stands a deliberate meter higher than the Washington Monument. It was built in 1982 with over 22,000 white granite blocks, one each for the number of days Kim had lived to date. Also finished that year was an Arch of Triumph, bigger and better than the one in Paris and marking the spot where he made a speech in liberated Korea after the Second World War. The humble home where he was born is a major tourist attraction, the other houses in the village long cleared away. Monuments dot the country where he or his family members allegedly performed a "brilliant exploit," communist-speak for serving the cause. Everywhere he gave his world famous "on-the-spot guidance," there's a commemorative plaque. Amazingly, he beat the non-existent competition to win the country's top awards, the Double Hero Gold Medal and Order of the National Banner, First Class, and established his own: the Kim Il-sung Medal, the Kim Il-sung Gold Medal and the

Kim Il-sung Youth Award. His birthday, April 15, has been North Korea's Christmas Day for decades. His face was more important than the country's flag, the "Song of General Kim Il-sung" more important than the national anthem.[3] It is, in short, the mother of all personality cults. You can't help wondering if such lunacy was not to make up for some withering insecurity.

We have to say, though, that one man couldn't pull this off on his own. There's a cultural factor to consider. North Korea is indeed an aberration, but, as offensive as this may seem to South Koreans, so many of its aspects are embarrassingly Korean. One such is the Korean habit of reverence for leaders.

Visualize this: in January 2003, senior executives of Hyundai Asan, the affiliate of the South Korean conglomerate which was pursuing founder Chung Ju-yung's dream of doing business in North Korea, went to Mr Chung's tomb to tell him they were opening the first road for tourists to travel into the North.[4] The happy report was made at exactly 5.50 a.m., the bad-breath hour at which the late Mr Chung used to hold his regular morning meetings. This deference to a man who in life would kick his executives in the shins and throw ashtrays at them was entirely of their choosing. But it made sense, partly because their new boss was the most filial of Mr Chung's sons, but more because loyalty touches the Korean soul deeper than a balance sheet. In South Korea, freedom, sophistication and competing loyalties serve to temper such cultishness. But in the North, it knows no bounds.

In North Korea, we should consider an additional factor: ignorance. There are no other heroes because people don't know about them, and there is no negative news about the Kims to temper the people's patriotic affection. Again, it requires some imagination to stand in North Koreans' shoes and appreciate their media environment. What they don't know about the modern world is astounding. On various visits, I searched in vain to find an ordinary North Korean who had heard of Elvis Presley or Michael Jackson. *Homo nordocoreanus* has not been informed that man has landed on the moon because that knowledge risks making him admire America.

Also, importantly, he doesn't really know much about the objects of worship, the two Kims. He's fed anecdotes and quotes, rather like Bible verses. Which raises an interesting comparison. The less one knows about a revered figure, the more difficult it is to strive to become like him or her, and the greater the tendency to place that person on a pedestal and worship from afar. So it is with Kim Il-sung. Born of heroic lineage, conductor of miracles, single-handed liberator of Korea from Japanese occupation, he is placed so impossibly high that all the subject can do is believe, worship, and proselytize. The call to express loyalty is louder than the call to embody his values (in other words, for personal development), which may explain why North Korea is an economic basket case.

Furthermore, there are no alternative heroes. No movie stars — North Korean films do not even have credits — pop musicians, writers, politicians, TV personalities, athletes. And, importantly, no ordinary heroes like firemen, cops, guys rowing across the Pacific, kids with cancer. Only Him. At school, you learn of His exploits and His love. Of how the Americans started the Korean War and He repelled them. (No one tells you that actually He started it. Only the elderly know and they keep quiet.) You study His Thought. At train stations, hymns about Him waft from loudspeakers and your homesickness and travel blues mix in with love for Him. Our unity around Him makes us a world power. One day He will free the poor children of South Korea. And when you take the otherworldly journey through His former palace till finally He is lying there before you, you feel unworthy. The suffering of our nation bursts from your heart and you bow sobbing. It's religion.

Just as other dictators of the modern age have linked to their mass audiences through ideology, so Kim Il-sung's system of thought underpinned his rule. It is called — what else? —

Kimilsung-joo-eui (Kimilsungism), but is better understood by its official name of *Juche* (self-reliance). In addition, there is fearsome repression. We shall get to both of these in later chapters, but for now we should note the most significant factor behind the cult of the man lying in the mausoleum in Pyongyang: the role of his son in its creation.

Koreans historically are known for fervor. Before producing the world's most fanatical and rigid communist cult, they had adopted Chinese Confucianism and its core value of filial piety in the most extreme form. South Korea boasts Asia's most devoted Christians and, if such a statistic could ever be measured, we'd probably find more heretic spin-offs and start-ups per head than anywhere else in the world. This curious energy seems to come from what we might call the shaman within the Korean psyche. Before Christianity, Confucianism or Buddhism, shaman-kings ruled Korean tribes. Their legacy remains in the Korean makeup. The shamans did not teach about contradictions such as good and evil or right and wrong, which tend to make you pause and think about your feelings and actions. They saw the individual as a whole, men and women as being of equal value, and each person's characteristics as equally valid. This "I'm-OK–you're-OK" approach provided the confidence to implement another shaman idea: that is, that life should be lived to the full. To be truly human, you must act with all your energies.[5]

The involvement of Kim Jong-il acting with all his energies provided the vital catalyst that made the cult of Kim Il-sung the most extreme in the communist world. In the early 1970s, for example, Kim Jong-il controlled the "4.15 Creation Group," named after Kim senior's April 15 birthday, which produced the immortal classics which the public was led to believe flowed directly from the Great Leader's own pen.[6] Kim Jong-il oversaw the building of the Juche Tower, the Arch of Triumph and the Kim Il-sung Stadium for his father's seventieth birthday.[7] This was how the son demonstrated to his father and the old revolutionaries around him that he was devoted to their cause and a worthy successor. It was also the means by which he was portrayed to the citizens as a nice, cuddly fellow, whose filial devotion was greater than theirs.

And it is also why Kim Jong-il became known as the "Dear Leader" (*chinae-haneun jidoja*).

For outsiders, the Dear Leader title is laughable. Indeed, it is hard for us to believe that the hand that writes such flaky propaganda belongs to one of the world's most ferocious regimes. So much of it has the character of a fairy tale, with the Dear Leader like a fairy in a tutu touching the small stuff of life with his magic wand. For example, back in 1965 the Dear Leader — who, according to the book, *The Great Teacher of Journalists: Kim Jong-il*, always sees everything "with an innovator's eye and [grasps] the developing reality and the aspirations of our people" — changed a radio signature tune. On his return from a "long trip to a far-off country, the dear leader came to inspect the Radio and TV Broadcasting Committee, without even stopping to break the longstanding fatigue of the journey abroad," and said:

> The character of our radio tune now in use is dull.
>
> Our broadcast is the voice of our Party which is guided by the leader, the voice of Juche Korea. So the signature tune which identifies the beginning of our radio programmes [*sic*: British spelling in North Korea] must naturally be a melody associated with the leader.
>
> It would be advisable to adopt as signature tune the melody of "Song of General Kim Il Sung," the immortal revolutionary hymn which is sung with feelings of high respect for him not only by our people but all the people throughout the world.[8]

As foreigners, we can only ever peer in at North Korea and try to make sense of it. I'd be the first to admit, though, that it is easy to misread what it's all about. Indeed, westerners misread the country all the time. The only time I was at Kumsusan I saw a couple of embarrassing displays of this.

It was for Kim Il-sung's eighty-second birthday in 1994. By that time, international Communism having collapsed, the foreign turn-out was so poor that the delegation I was in, which included a former premier of Egypt and a former governor-general of Canada, provided the festivities' main VIPs and got invited to lunch. This group also included representatives from CNN, the Japanese TV network NHK, and three from *The Washington Times*, for which I was writing at the time. When the twenty or so members lined up to shake the Hand, the reporter in me decided to stand instead near the GL (Great Leader) and take pictures. I got close up as each VIP had a brief exchange. One, an American academic, had met him once before and obviously thought they were great friends. When it was his turn, he leaned back dramatically, spread his arms wide, leaving the proffered Hand hanging there for a moment, and exclaimed, "You look great!" Kim Il-sung maintained his gracious composure, but I swear a shadow flitted across his eyes as he wondered, "Who the hell are you?" Not only did this Washington-like familiarity seem off the mark, but so was the observation about his health, for two months later the GL was dead.

The second scene was more protracted. We lunched around a large circular table, enjoying quail egg soup and donkey meat. The GL was a gracious host, if rather stuck in the past, referring on several occasions to Korea's struggle for independence from Japan and to the Korean War, albeit with polite apologies to his Japanese and American guests. I wondered if the Queen always reminds visitors that England thrashed the Germans in two world wars and in the final of the 1966 World Cup. A representative from CNN rose to speak. A pitch for an interview was imminent. Our newspaper had already secured an interview of sorts — written answers to questions — and I had competitive fingers crossed under the table that CNN's effort would be turned down.

"Sir, I bring you greetings from Ted Turner and Jane Fonda," he said. ("He brings greetings from his leader and wife, who is an actress," the interpreter said in Korean.) His speech was good, very diplomatic and, sure enough, ended with an interview request.

"I am glad you are enjoying your visit to our country," the GL replied. There was a pause during which you could hear foreign brains failing to figure that this was his one and final answer.

"Sir, CNN is available in 200 countries and territories around the world…" came a reworded attempt. It was politely declined. Someone else had another go. This was getting painful. Then the academic jumped in. Another decline. I should have been sensing victory for the international brotherhood of print journalists, but instead was squirming as a fellow westerner. Attempt number five: the academic stood up, reached into his jacket, and whipped out a sheet of paper.

"Mr President, I have in my hand a map of the world, showing all the spots where people can see CNN. I'd like to give this to you." Oh no, he was leaning across two people, including a senior Party secretary, and handing this thing to the dictator. I had to stop myself biting my knuckles. "For your consideration, and should you…"

"I have no desire to throw myself upon the world," Kim Il-sung said and, finally, everyone got it.

He talked with pride about how he'd built up the country. Frankly, North Korea was a dump to western eyes, but for a micro-manager, as dictators tend to be, there was a lot to be proud of — and it was affirmed by all the tributes to him his son was building. He was proud of his honest and disciplined people and recounted how a foreign visitor who had lost his wallet in a hotel had it returned to him at the airport as he was leaving. He proudly explained how his workers' revolution was not just a hammer-and-sickle affair. "I knew intellectuals were vital," he said, explaining why a pen is included in the North Korean emblem. Maybe he thought he was reassuring us as we scribbled away that our own lives could have meaning. We were not personally afraid of him, of course. We were kind of pinching ourselves at the sheer luck of being in the presence of a man that journalists had been trying to interview for decades. Rather, in the way that scholars and journalists, and sometimes movie stars, are awed by the powerful and often do their vile bidding, we were rolling over and letting him tickle us.

"Mr President, what do you do for leisure?" someone asked. The GL explained how he enjoyed hunting and fishing, but that now he was getting too old for it.

"Soldiers raise bears for me to hunt, but I think that now they hide behind a tree with a tame bear and push it out when I come along," he said, making a dictator-joke against himself which would have gone down a treat at an NRA dinner.

On the way out, he shook hands with us again. I told him in Korean that I was the Seoul correspondent for my paper, half expecting he'd ask me to stay for tea to hear his life story. But, up close, he seemed rather distracted, and didn't appear to take this important news in. I later learned that, by then, he was unable to contain his flatulence, and I wonder now whether maybe at that very moment he was struggling to hold in a big one.[9]

There then occurred a minor incident which spoke more volumes than anything else. The penultimate figure in the greeting line was the Korean-American consultant who had arranged the trip. The GL knew her, considered her a "foreigner," and so welcomed her with a smile. The luncheon was, after all, with foreigners who had come to "celebrate" his birthday. Our relative informality and freedom to question him was clearly not something that his own people ever enjoyed. In fact, every time Kim Il-sung addressed one of the North Korean officials, they had to put down their cutlery and stand up when they replied. Anyway, the Hand then went out for the last person.

When he saw who it was — the lady's North Korean business partner — the Hand dropped and the Great Leader turned away with a scowl, leaving the hapless fellow to ponder his faux pas.[10]

One notable personal feature of Kim Il-sung was the massive, grenade-sized goiter on the back of his neck. You might think this rather startling apparition would have served as a permanent reminder to his subjects that this man was just another flawed human being, but that would be to miss a key factor in Korean obedience. In general terms, for Americans, it's tough to worship someone unless he or she is unreal, preferably long dead, and who thereby exhibits no human flaws. The Japanese, by contrast, tend to not see the flaws and so can follow as if the actual person is divine. The Koreans, however, see the flaws very clearly, but can still follow. The god they follow is human and they'll use PR to cover up his flaws because they have a stake in his continuing success. Life, they understand, is not a matter of striving for affirmation from a loving god, but rather a question of appeasing fickle spirits and people with power, and dodging their tantrums in order to get on.

Initially, The Thing, which was benign, was surgically removed in the propaganda photos, but in later years, it was let be. When we had the pre-lunch interview session with the GL, though, a guard stood on the offending side to block the photographers. You wonder whether the security folk planned this deployment using a code-name for it, or whether its existence was always denied.

Kim Jong-il was nowhere to be seen at this time, although he kindly sent baskets of fruit to our rooms. In fact, by then he was effectively running the country. Kim Il-sung told us that his eyes were bad and that his son had taken to providing him with daily taped reports of affairs of state.

JI's style, however, was to remain in the background. He never spoke in public and seldom turned up to meet foreigners. On one rare occasion, Russian reporters told me, he arrived with his father to a New Year reception for foreign diplomats. He gave an impression of being ill at ease and had a hard time smiling naturally. "Kim Il-sung was gracious as usual," recalled Alexandr Zhebin, the TASS correspondent in Pyongyang at the time. But the Dear Leader had an awkward smile on his face and looked "as if he had swallowed poison." As such perceptions filtered out, analysts overseas speculated that perhaps Kim Jong-il suffered from shyness. Perhaps he stuttered. Or maybe he had mental problems.

In fact, the low profile was Kim Jong-il's survival strategy. Contrary to assumed wisdom, Kim Jong-il was not a shoe-in as the successor. It's my understanding from North Korean explanations that Kim Il-sung's prime loyalty was not to his family but to his revolution and that if Kim Jong-il had not proved himself worthy, he would have been passed over. That he avoided upstaging his father — a potential successor always draws attention from an incumbent — and that he built all the monuments tells us something about his father and the revolution. The two were inseparable in the old man's mind. And his ability in recognizing this and acting accordingly for twenty years as heir apparent says something about Kim Jong-il's survival instincts.

Which brings us to the present.

North Korea is a state in profound trouble and, although the ruling Korean Workers' Party remains formally committed to communizing the whole peninsula, JI's policies are aimed toward one end: the survival of both himself and his country. As a communist state, North Korea is a political dinosaur at odds with the civilized world. Isolated, paranoid, the leadership has lost the race with the rival South; and it continues to resist the tutelage of its ally, China, and the willingness of its neighbors, including the South, to help. As a result, the state is bankrupt. Yet, through stubborn pride and fear of failure, and with a ruthless internal system of suppression still at its disposal, the regime hangs on.

You'd expect JI would want to do something to improve things. But when he tries, there's an element of buffoonery that forecasts failure. Examples: on a rare visit to the US, a high-ranking Party leader proposes that Washington and Pyongyang unite as a bulwark against Japan. A weird blaze of publicity around its appointment of a foreign tycoon to head a free zone near the Chinese border ends with the tycoon's arrest in China.

For their ability to run a twenty-first century state, North Korea's leaders may as well be from outer space, a theme *The Economist* touched on when it captioned a cover picture of a waving Kim Jong-il, "Greetings, Earthlings." And they've sealed their borders and turned off the landing lights so that the prosecutors from their home planet can't spot them.

Maybe that explains the darkness.

2

Two States, One Rose

None of present-day North Korea makes sense without reference to its historic rivalry with South Korea. This started in 1945, immediately after the Second World War, when the Soviet Union and the United States drew a dividing line between their own zones of influence in Korea along the thirty-eighth parallel, and favored rival groups among independence activists. By 1948, communists on one side and pro-western figures on the other had formed separate countries. Each one claimed to be the real Korea and each was dedicated to a future reunified Korea under its control. Just which side would eventually win was anybody's guess. They were like two suitors trying to appeal to the bachelorette of history. Two states, one rose. Who would be left broken-hearted and with their egos shattered?

For some time now, the winner has been clear. It's South Korea.

We may wish to be neutral and hope there is some contribution from the North to the structure of a future Unified Korea. But there is none. North Korea will come with minerals, land, cheap labor and a sad and bewildered generation to take care of. There may be a nuclear weapons program, too, but the South would have to dismantle it. North Korea will bring nothing conceptual, nothing in terms of political or economic theory, for it is a shambolic dictatorship whose existence serves to remind us in the twenty-first century, lest we forget, of the utter intellectual and organizational madness Communism represented in the twentieth.

Civilization seems to have settled the argument as to how it wishes to structure itself: a developed society must be law-based, politically democratic and economically free-market, with religion a personal rather than a state choice. Regardless of whether this is right or desirable and regardless of whether it may change in the future, that's the system that's out there for now. No nation has developed without embracing it, except perhaps some city-states like Singapore and some in the Gulf, which withhold the democratic part. This is a reality that South Korea vigorously embodies and that North Korea, to its peril, has resisted. For this reason, Unified Korea will be an expanded South Korea.

Within South Korea itself, there is opposition to this idea from some nationalists who think that the South's early reliance on the "imperialistic" United States for security and aid disqualifies it. These people, who lean politically leftward, are more willing to look at the two Koreas as equals and to believe that their union will create a third, superior being. They remind us that in the 1940s, the two Koreas went at each other like gangsters. Both, for example, were shocking on human rights. But that was then. Now the South is an honest businessman. The northern thug has been cornered up a dead-end street and its long-standing rival and the American cop are trying to persuade him to drop his weapon.

How did it get to this?

That question takes us back a long way.

The Koreans have been Korean for several thousand years.[1] The first thing foreign visitors learn is that the country has been around for an official "5,000 years". Koreans are believed to descend from Neolithic groups which came into the peninsula between 5500 B.C. and 2000 B.C., and from Bronze Age clans which arrived around 1,000 years later, possibly from the Altaic speakers of central Asia. From that point they have been homogeneous and distinct, culturally and linguistically, from their neighbors.

The founding father, Tangun, was, according to legend, the product of the mating of a god and a bear, which we can be thankful wasn't caught on video. Born in 2333 B.C., shortly after the fall of Jericho, he apparently built the walled city of Pyongyang and called his territory in the northwest of the peninsula "Joseon," meaning, "Land of the Morning Calm." North Korean scholars in the 1990s unearthed an old tomb, which they claimed was Tangun's. South Koreans dispute the alleged find. They know very clearly what their communist neighbors are up to: laying claim to history, as if there's an unbroken line from Tangun to Kim Jong-il. This may seem an unusual thing for communists to do, but it is important for North Koreans because — unlike, say, the Chinese communist revolutionaries who swept the past away — they are nationalists whose objective was to free the country from Japanese colonialism. They sought to reclaim ownership of Korea rather than to change it.

For good reason. Korea had been a single state since the year 936 when the various chiefdoms were united along what is roughly the current territory of North and South (the precise current border of North Korea and China dates to the fifteenth century). The dynasty at that time was called "Koryo," whence the name "Korea." Its capital was Kaesong[2] in today's North Korea, which is why the North's longstanding proposal for reunification with the South is for a "Koryo Federation." In 1392, this dynasty was ousted in a military coup, after which the new regime revived the old name, Joseon. North Korea retains this word, rendering it "Chosun" in their English transliteration. ("Joseon" is the South Korean spelling.)

The coup came with a Confucian revolution. One of its ideas was the "Mandate of Heaven," by which legitimacy derives from divine backing. Heaven signals its withdrawal through natural disasters, poor harvests, and military defeats. (Two down, one to go for Kim Jong-il.) The Confucian revolutionaries set up a caste system of five classes headed by a scholarly upper stratum of civilian and military officials known as *yangban*, whose aspirations were to government service and learning. Under them were the *chung-in* or "middle people" — doctors, translators, clerks and the like — followed by commoners (*sang-in*), such as craftspeople, farmers and merchants who made up half the population. Peasants in this category were restricted by law from leaving their land and had to carry identity papers at all times. They were organized into groups of five families responsible for keeping an eye on each other. Moving down the ladder, you would find folks like gravediggers and butchers whose jobs were passed down from father to son. They made up the *chonmin* or "inferior people," and lived in separate villages or scraped by as gypsies. Finally, a sizeable number of people — even going into the twentieth century — were slaves, a feature of their history modern Koreans prefer to ignore. Some kind of similar caste structure operates in North Korea today, with people classified according to their presumed degree of loyalty to the communist revolution.

Another feature of modern North Korea — its isolation — has echoes in history. Korea was always seen as a remote place, and in the mid-nineteenth century it sought to avoid the problems that China had suffered with western imperialists and closed off, earning it the title "the Hermit Kingdom". Finally, in the early 1880s (over protests from conservatives), King Kojong, through Chinese mediation, opened ties with America, and then Britain, Germany, Italy, Russia, France, and Austria–Hungary.

Around this time, Japan was a rising power. Its strategy in order to avoid falling victim to western imperialism was to become a regional imperialist itself. In 1904, it defeated Russia in a war during which Japanese troops occupied Seoul and never left. Formal annexation came in 1910 and 14.7 million Koreans became Japanese with hardly a shot fired. Japanese became the official language. The governor-general built his offices in front of the royal palace, blocking it from public view. Metal stakes were driven into hilltops to kill what Koreans believed was the country's spiritual energy. Later, too, Koreans were forced to worship at Shinto shrines and adopt Japanese names. Youngsters lost touch with their heritage and bought into Japanese assumptions of Korean inferiority.

And so a peasant people, locked for centuries into backwardness by fear of spirits and by a caste system presided over by a scholarly class who spurned innovation and for whom imitation of past classics was the most virtuous use of creativity, was brought kicking into the modern world as subjects of the Japanese.

The most notable resistance to Japanese rule came in 1919, when 33 religious nationalists signed a declaration of independence and called for peaceful demonstrations. The Japanese reacted savagely, killing several thousand as they suppressed the largely peaceful protests. Politically, this independence effort achieved nothing, but it awoke Koreans to their identity and, in this sense, from its bloody womb the modern Korean twins were born.

Disunity characterized the independence activists. They fell into broad camps of nationalists, who either built schools and businesses or went into exile, and others who turned to the new ideas of Marxist-Leninism. The sad fact is that these groups made little contribution to Korea's eventual liberation, which came with the defeat of Japan by allied forces in 1945.

The United States and the Soviet Union, a late entrant into the Pacific War, had agreed to take the Japanese surrender in Korea on either side of the thirty-eighth parallel. In its zone —

the South — the United States rather unthinkingly dismantled a nationwide network of what were known as People's Committees, formed by activists and respected local figures in the weeks before the US troops arrived, and installed an American military government, which actually retained some Japanese officials and police to help with administration. The Americans backed an elderly conservative, Rhee Syngman, who had lived in exile for 40 years, as their man. The Soviets brought in a young officer in a Red Army uniform called Kim Il-sung.

The eldest of three sons of Christian peasants, Kim was born on April 15, 1912, in a village called Man-gyong-dae near Pyongyang.[3] His parents named him Song-ju. His father, Kim Hyeong-jik, was an oriental medicine practitioner, and had been educated at a school founded by American missionaries. His mother, Kang Pan-seok, was a church deacon. When he was seven, the family moved to Manchuria. Seven years later, his father died aged 32. The young Kim lived in China until he was 28, aside from two years back in Korea in his early teens. Fluent in Mandarin, Kim was drawn to Communism and expelled from school in China for this involvement. His first arrest came in the fall of 1929, in the city of Jilin, where he experienced "finger-breaking torture."[4] Although unconvincingly written up — "While in prison, I pondered over the way to lead the Korean revolution" — jail was clearly a defining experience for the 17 year-old, and after release he left his family to follow the guerrillas.[5]

After one of his comrades wrote a song about him, *Star of Korea,* they started calling him "Han Byol" (One Star). But the night is full of stars, and soon they were calling him "Il Sung" (Be The Sun), as one whom they hoped would help save Koreans from the darkness of Japanese rule. The second nom de guerre stuck, over his apparent protests. "I did not like to be called by another name. Still less did I tolerate the people extolling me by comparing me to a star or the sun; it did not befit me, [a] young man. But my comrades would not listen to me, no matter how sternly I rebuked them."[6]

In 1931, Be The Sun joined the Chinese Communist Party, which was Korean-dominated in Manchuria, and in the following year began his career as an anti-Japanese guerrilla with the Chinese National Salvation Army. Shortly after, he was arrested and eventually cleared by Chinese communists in an extensive purge of alleged pro-Japanese Koreans in which several hundred were executed. After this nasty introduction to Communism in action, in June 1934 he joined the Northeast Anti-Japanese United Army, which was under Chinese command. He led a unit of up to 300 men who conducted mostly hit-and-run raids on Japanese police and other targets in Manchuria and northern Korea. Apparently he kidnapped boys to join his unit. He fundraised by offering protection services to ginseng and opium farmers and by extorting rich Koreans, often taking hostages and threatening to cut off their heads. Kim was notable not only for becoming the most wanted man in Manchuria, but also for his perseverance.[7] While most other revolutionaries were killed, captured or turned, Kim survived, fleeing to the Soviet Union in late 1940, when the Japanese destroyed the guerrillas in China. There, the Korean partisans were eventually restructured as the 88th Special Reconnaissance Brigade of the Soviet 25th (Far Eastern) Army, led by a Chinese commander. Kim Il-sung headed one of its four battalions, which undertook reconnaissance and infiltration activities. He was now a Red Army officer and saw himself as part of the larger international Soviet-led struggle against imperialism. By 1945, 33-year-old Captain Kim was a leading figure among the Manchurian guerrilla faction in the Soviet Far East.

Two days after the Hiroshima bomb, the Soviet Union declared war on Japan and a week later Japan surrendered. As previously agreed, the Red Army moved through Manchuria into North Korea. Undisciplined Soviet soldiers upset the liberated locals in North Korea with their rape and pillage — a favorite trick was bumping peasants out of the way with their jeeps.[8] The Soviets did not intend to form a government in the North as the Americans had done in the South. Instead, they sought to install Captain Kim as their man. Soviet political officers found Kim Il-sung confident, affable, and self-disciplined. He nevertheless surveyed his new landscape with the eyes of a guerrilla, unexposed to urban life, suspicious of the world, hardened by years of struggle, and accustomed to an environment of cruelty and criminality.[9]

Although uneducated, Kim was savvy enough to know that his record needed some spin-doctoring. He asked the chief Soviet political officer to help make it look as though the anti-Japanese partisans had played a role in the liberation of Korea.[10] This appeal was unsuccessful, but the Soviets were soon to realize that their boy needed some work. In October 1945, they arranged a mass rally in Pyongyang to welcome Captain Kim as a returning hero. As Kim read the speech written for him by a Soviet official and translated by a Korean poet, many among the 300,000 in the crowd began to yell abuse. They could not believe that the young fellow in a suit and sporting a Soviet medal was actually Kim Il-sung the legendary guerilla fighter.[11] Soviet authorities then undertook an image campaign that led directly to the mind-boggling personality cult that remains intact 60 years later.

The US and Soviet allies originally figured that Korea would need a US–USSR trusteeship, like that imposed on Austria. But Korean opposition to the proposed five-year occupation began the lurch toward permanent division. As left and right polarized, violence seared the South, and Christians, landowners and other non-communists streamed out of the North. Elections sponsored by the newly formed United Nations in 1948 were blocked in the North, but went ahead in the South and led to the formation of a separate state, the pro-American Republic of Korea, whose first president was Rhee Syngman. Three weeks later, the North formed the pro-Soviet Democratic People's Republic of Korea with Kim Il-sung at the helm.[12]

So why, we may wonder, did political leaders in such a homogenous society not make that extra effort to insist on a unified structure? Koreans on both sides would say that their leaders were helpless to prevent the Americans and Soviets from dividing them. But that's only half the story. They were not browbeaten into division by Washington and Moscow. Rather, political leaders lacked a strong sense of national identity and felt justified in harnessing superpower support for their personal and factional ambitions. Disunity was their undoing. It may seem ironic, therefore, that reunification became the mantra on both sides. But what the rival governments meant by being dedicated to reunification was that they had sole claim to legitimacy and considered the other side to be "rebel-held." So, "unification" actually means the reclaiming of lost territory.

Before you can "unify," you have to solidify your base, which, given the mistrust and propensity for fractiousness, means cracking skulls. Kim Il-sung was good at this and pretty soon was ready for a real shot at unification. On June 25, 1950, with Stalin's go-ahead, his tanks rumbled across the border and within three days were in Seoul, a rapidity that somehow makes it difficult to believe the North's claim that it was attacked first. After a few weeks, his communist forces had liberated the entire country, with the exception of the area around the southeast port of Busan.[13]

But Kim made two miscalculations in his bid for unification. The first was that he thought, or had been led to believe by South Korean communists, that the people in the South would welcome him. They didn't. The "good behavior" of North Korean soldiers — they did not on the whole get boozed up and slap women around — somehow didn't make up for the rounding up and massacring of property-owners and churchgoers. The other mistake was to assume that the

Americans wouldn't help the South Koreans. They did. And they weren't the only ones. Suddenly North Korea found itself fighting South Koreans, the United States, and Britain, Australia, Belgium, Canada, Colombia, Ethiopia, France, Greece, Luxembourg, the Netherlands, New Zealand, the Philippines, South Africa, Thailand, and Turkey, with non-combatant support from Denmark, India, Italy, Norway, and Sweden.

But it was too late to turn back.

Kim's army was dissected and routed when the allied forces, fighting for the first time under the United Nations flag, counter-invaded. In a plan conceived by the UN commander, the legendary US General Douglas MacArthur, the Americans landed at the western port city of Incheon,[14] pounded their way into Seoul and handed the capital back to the South Korean government.

The South and its backers then made a miscalculation of their own when they failed to anticipate the willingness of Mao Tse-tung, whose communists had taken control of China the year before, to join the fray. When United Nations units raced across the border and swept up as far as the Yalu River on the border with China, Mao's forces swept into Korea and pushed rapidly south.

By the time the armistice was signed in July 1953, the two sides had settled along roughly the same frontline as when they'd started, except that Kaesong was now in the North. The toll was staggering. Civilian casualties: three million. North Korean, South Korean and Chinese soldiers dead and wounded: almost two million. Allied dead: over 33,000 Americans, 1,000 British, and 4,000 other nationalities. Among the living, there were hundreds of thousands of orphans and widows, millions homeless and millions who would be permanently separated from closest family by the demilitarized zone that separated the two armies.

The agony of the Korean War is slowly receding, but the blood-soaked legacy of the most extreme of all national divisions remains.

Kim Il-sung should have lost his job after the armistice, but the Great Survivor purged rivals, tightened the bolts on his centralized power system, and turned up the volume on the personality cult — and with it the wee fib that he had saved the country from a war started by the United States — to ensure lifelong power. US troops remained in the South, protecting the fragile and increasingly repressive regime of Syngman Rhee, and providing Kim with a ready argument that the South was a "puppet state." In 1960, the Americans suggested that Rhee leave office after student protests. A parliamentary democracy was introduced under Prime Minister Chang Myun, but this government was shunted aside without protest nine months later by a bloodless military coup.[15]

The new leader, Park Chung-hee, was not a liberal-democrat. He had been a Japanese army officer in Manchuria and, in liberated Korea, was drawn to the political left by his brother, a communist. In 1948, a military tribunal had sentenced him to death for his role in a leftist riot, but then commuted the sentence after Park turned against communists. It is not clear which came first, the commuting or the change of sides, but this resume was enough to alarm the Kennedy administration, which feared for a while that the Reds had taken power. But Park turned out to be an anti-communist kind of communist, a fascist if you like, in a way that demonstrates that these kinds of labels are not always useful.

While Rhee had waffled in the 1950s about "marching north," South Korea did not present much of a threat to the North, either militarily or in terms of undermining North Korea's claim as the legitimate Korea. The arrival of Park, however, changed that. In reaction to the corruption of the Rhee government and its dependency on the United States, Park set about building an industrial base upon which a future Korea could sustain its defense with or without American support. He took the historic step of normalizing relations with Japan. Highly unpopular at the time, this initiative buried a self-destructive hatchet and brought in loans. Park also raised the country's military profile by sending troops to fight along-side US forces in Vietnam, after which the United States awarded lucrative contracts to young Korean companies.

In the decades following the war, with both sides ruled by soldiers in civilian clothes, the Cold War was never colder than it was in Korea. A four-kilometer-wide no-man's-land separated the two Koreas, a demilitarized zone filled with mines and, deep underneath, North Koreans digging secret tunnels. "There ain't no 'D' in that 'MZ'," as one US commander in the South used to say. No traffic crossed the eerie wasteland. The only meeting point in the middle, a collection of buildings called Panmunjom, where North Korean and American guards stared balefully at each other, became East Asia's Cold War motif. Both governments forbade their citizens from freely discussing the unification question and the most harmless interest in the other side could be considered treasonous. In the 1970s, for example, South Korean stamp collectors might get arrested if they got a hold of DPRK stamps (sad because there are some great ones. A particular favorite of mine is a North Korean stamp celebrating the 1981 wedding of Prince Charles and Lady Diana.)

The South has moved on since then but, as we shall see, the North hasn't, which is why stamp collectors and history will forgive Park his anti-democratic ways. By the time of his 1979 assassination (by his own intelligence chief), Park had transformed South Korea's ragged folk into shipbuilders and carmakers. Per capita income was US$82 when Park took power in 1961 and reached US$10,000 by 1997. Park was not a democrat. But his economic miracle spawned a political miracle after his death. In the 1980s, democracy was squeezed out of his generation of leaders for whom it represented "chaos." In 1988, Roh Tae-woo was installed as South Korea's first democratically elected president.

As South Korea was developing, Kim Il-sung tried every option to "unify" and failed. Although it is unlikely the Great Leader ever contemplated a repeat of the 1950 invasion, the US-South Korean Combined Forces Command structure has always been deployed to deter it. Another factor was that Kim would no longer have had Chinese or Soviet help for a second shot. With the denouncement of Stalin in 1956, North Korea's ties with the Soviet Union became strained. North Korea tried to maintain neutrality during the Sino-Soviet dispute, but for the crime of ignoring the Cultural Revolution of the mid-1960s, China's Red Guards went for him, describing him as a "fat counter-revolutionary pig" who lived in five palaces. The Red Guards, who weren't noted for accurate reporting, may have exaggerated on the number of palaces. When we consider that China is North Korea's closest ally, it is remarkable to recall the extent of the rift at the time, and it makes the 2002 anti-American demonstrations in Seoul seem like a friendly discussion. Even before the fat pig article in the Red Guards' journal, ambassadors were recalled, Chinese officers withdrew from the Military Armistice Commission overseeing the peace in Panmunjom, and loudspeakers allegedly blared anti-Chinese propaganda across the border.[16]

By the time North Korea's relations with the two communist superpowers had improved, the Great Leader had already turned his attention to the Third World, where he would make a failed effort to become the leader of the Non-Aligned Movement. The chilling with Moscow and Beijing had another significant effect in that it led to the development of *Juche*, Kim's ideology of self-reliance, and to an intensification of the personality cult. The North Koreans then airbrushed the Soviet liberation of Korea and the Chinese rescue during the Korean War out of history.

Also at this time, Kim Il-sung's fellow partisans took prominent posts. This led to North Korea taking a more aggressive military posture, which the Great Leader did not resist. The decision was made in 1962, after failure to secure military aid from Moscow, to strengthen defense at the expense of the economy. Thus began the militarization of the entire society.

In January 1968, the partisans sent a special commando squad into South Korea with the mission of cutting off President Park's head by February 8, the twentieth anniversary of the founding of the (North) Korean People's Army.[17] The guerrillas, whose training included scooping out graves and sleeping next to the skeletons, made it to within a stone's throw of the presidential Blue House before being stopped. Twenty-seven were killed, two escaped, and two were captured, one of whom blew himself up with a hidden grenade. The sole survivor, named Kim Shin-jo, received letters in prison from some Korean Christian girls, married one of them when he was released and went on to become a Presbyterian preacher.[18] North Korean propaganda alleged the whole incident was a domestic revolutionary effort by South Koreans and followed it up through that year with several incursions by commando units, all of which ended in failure.

A few days after the failed Blue House attack, North Korean naval forces came across the USS Pueblo, an intelligence ship, and despite protests by its captain, Lloyd "Pete" Bucher, that his vessel was in international waters, seized it, killing one member of the 83-man crew. This incident produced a classic of American POW defiance when North Koreans triumphantly released a propaganda photo of several captured crew members surreptitiously giving the camera the finger. Bucher signed a confession that he'd been spying in North Korean waters after being told his crew would be executed one by one, starting with the youngest, until he did. The Americans were finally released in December of that year. For his confession and for failing to fend off the North Korean navy with the two machine guns he had on board, Bucher was recommended for court martial by a naval inquiry, a move nixed by the Navy Secretary. The ship has for years been a tourist site in the North Korean port of Wonsan. North Korean officials were reportedly preparing to return it to the US in 2002 in a gesture of peace, when they were pre-empted by Washington's exposure of Pyongyang's enriched uranium program.[19]

The partisan generals' guerrilla adventures proved a disaster, and almost brought the country to war with the United States. The generals also posed a potential threat to Kim Il-sung, so from the end of 1968 he started to purge them. He gave up guerrilla activity against South Korea, although different forms of aggression, combining military action, espionage and political subversion, continued. The following spring, on Kim Il-sung's birthday in 1969, North Korean MiG-21s shot down a US Navy spy plane with 31 crew on board. In June 1970, three North Korean agents tried to plant a bomb at the gate of the National Cemetery where Park was scheduled to give a speech marking the twentieth anniversary of the outbreak of the war. The bomb went off as they were planting it, killing one. The other two fled but were later found and killed. In 1974, South Koreans stumbled upon an elaborate invasion tunnel dug under the DMZ. (Others would be discovered in 1975, 1978 and 1990. Defectors say there may be as many as 16 more.) In the same year, a Japanese-born North Korean agent shot at Park, but missed. Bodyguards fired back and someone's bullets killed the first lady and a choirgirl.

In between these second and third assassination attempts, Kim, alarmed by the Sino-US rapprochement, initiated a peace offensive to which Park, who never trusted that US support would continue, responded. Significantly, on July 4, 1972, the two rivals issued a joint declaration pledging peaceful efforts towards unity, in which neither leader believed. In October, Park conducted another coup of sorts, dissolving the National Assembly, and introducing martial law in a bid, the US embassy figured, to stay in power forever.

Another option to take over the South lay in political subversion which, had the North Koreans been better at it, might have yielded fruit over time, considering so many South Korean intellectuals felt their own side had less nationalistic legitimacy than the North for its obsequious dependency on the United States. One notable effort involved the formation of the Revolutionary Party for Reunification by a South Korean communist called Kim Chong-tae, at the prompting of North Korean agents. Kim had been busy for a few years and built up a network of intellectuals, but was discovered by the Korean CIA during the period of heightened surveillance following the failed 1974 assassination attempt, and executed. There have been numerous incidents since, involving special operations and spies. But the failure of North Korea to seriously figure during the sustained protests against the dictatorship of another coup-making president, Chun Doo-hwan, in the South in the 1980s, and even after many radical students had taken to illegally studying Kim's *Juche* ideas, is indication that its ability to unify by force or subversion had long disappeared.

While the North became weaker and weaker, the South went from strength to strength. The symbolic moment of South Korea's ascendancy came in 1981 when Seoul was awarded the right to host the 1988 Summer Olympics. The South Korean capital had seven years to prepare for the Games. With South Korea awash in tear gas through most of the 1980s, the International Olympic Committee had plenty of occasion to regret its decision. But the populace was solidly behind the Olympics. Twenty years of urban plans were telescoped and Chun made his closest ally and fellow coup-maker, Roh Tae-woo, head of the Seoul Olympic Organizing Committee. When in 1987 Chun announced that Roh was his party's presidential candidate for the December election, ordinary Koreans, fearing Roh would be shoed in through the government-manipulated electoral college, took to the streets to demand a constitutional change to allow for a direct popular vote. Street protests bringing out the bankers and the housewives lasted for three weeks and threatened to jeopardize the following year's Olympics. Roh himself called for a direct popular vote and Chun conceded.

In that same year, two North Korean agents posing as a Japanese father and daughter placed a bomb on a South Korean airliner. The agents were told the order had come directly from Kim Jong-il, who had by now emerged as the heir apparent in Pyongyang. The plan, they believed, was to make it look like domestic terrorism and create a security pretext for Pyongyang's communist allies to stay away from the Games.[20] The agents were caught in Bahrain, where they had disembarked after the first leg of the flight. The man swallowed a poison capsule and died, but the woman was brought to Seoul on the eve of the presidential vote, helping to swing it in Roh's favor. Thus exposed, Pyongyang lost the backing of its allies, who elected to come to Seoul, thereby ending a run of Olympic boycotts.

The Olympics Games themselves were magnificently staged. Although remembered for the disqualification of the Canadian sprinter, Ben Johnson, for drug use and for Carl Lewis' four golds, these Games also marked the moment that the world acknowledged the real Korea. Within four years, as Communism collapsed, the eastern European states, Russia and China all formed diplomatic relations with the South.

The rest should have been history.

3

Going Nuclear

T he seasons in Seoul are something to behold. The city itself has sprawled across the wide river and around the wooded hills that once lay outside its walls. A climate, similar to that of the northeast United States, colors its hills. I live on the slope of one of the steeper ones. The view when I open my eyes in the morning is of downtown, a 15-minute walk away. From the bathroom window to the east, I can see the presidential Blue House. It was from the crags that loom above the neighborhood that Kim Shin-jo and his fellow commandoes, on their mission in 1968 to kill President Park, got their first panoramic view of the enemy capital. The startling contrast of this to the war-wrecked images of North Korean propaganda worked in his heart, starting a process, he later said, which made him surrender to South Korean soldiers. Had he done as he had been trained, he would have committed suicide as the troops closed in on him.[1]

Since then, young men on military service have been discreetly deployed to watch the hikers on the city's popular routes. Their presence stirs the imagination. I sometimes wonder, when I'm walking my dog in these hills before breakfast, whether the old ladies filling their plastic bottles with natural spring water or the men doing barking exercises to expel their stale air — "Aaaaaaaaaahoooo!" — might not be highly trained communist agents. I doubt the dog, an American cocker spaniel, would be much use to me.

I've tried to envision missiles flying overhead and smacking into downtown, but can't quite see it. But I'm glad some experts can, because there are a lot of them not very far away.

Seoul is only around 40 miles from the DMZ. That's a commute — San Jose to San Francisco, less than Brighton up to London. Given this proximity, you wonder why the capital has been allowed to grow as it has. After Tokyo–Yokohama and New York City–Newark, Seoul forms with Incheon and Songnam the world's third largest agglomeration. Its 21 million inhabitants represent to the North Korean regime what Americans represent to al-Qaeda — the living opposition to everything they stand for. Of course, Kim Jong-il could deliver his special forces or lob a chemical load at them in no time. But, he has consequences to consider and can't duck and weave like a terrorist. There are assets he fears losing, a state to run, mouths to feed. Well, some mouths. And there are statue-builders, propaganda artists and prison guards to keep busy.

And lots of soldiers. The communist regime has always drawn its legitimacy from opposition to the South and to the United States, and as a result it has had to remain well armed and threatened by enemies to justify itself. As the United States and South Korea built their defenses, so North Korea felt further threatened. North Korea, as a state, shakes its fist at the world. It is a country, you might say, scared from within and from without. For reasons of this dynamic, North Korea has taken pains to remain, despite its backwardness in almost all else, internationally competitive in its ability to wage war.

On paper, the North Koreans have greater manpower, armor and artillery than the South. Ground forces number over one million, making them the world's third-biggest army.[2] The air force has 110,000 personnel with over 1,600 aircraft. The navy has 60,000 people and over 800 vessels, a huge fleet. In terms of numbers, the total force is the fifth in the world. The regime can call on reserves of over six million. Compulsory military service takes a decade out of a young man's life, and seven years from a young woman's.[3] Kim Jong-il spends only US$5.1 billion per year on defense, less than half South Korea's defense budget, but this amount represents a staggering 31.3 percent of the country's GDP.[4] This small country of only 22 million is the most militarized nation in the world.

US intelligence tells us that 70 percent of Kim Jong-il's ground forces are deployed within 100 miles of the DMZ. These forward troops are believed to have 2,000 tanks and 8,000 artillery systems, many of them hidden in some 4,000 underground facilities. At their disposal are 12,000 self-propelled and towed weapons systems and 500 long-range systems. If this formidable force were unleashed, the South would hardly have enough advanced warning to duck. Seoul's ability to respond would be seriously confounded by perhaps the scariest component of Kim's army, his special forces. These 90,000 or so highly trained troops, one of the largest such contingents in the world, would be delivered, quietly and rapidly, via tunnels under the DMZ and by submarine and small craft along the coast, and, dressed in South Korean uniforms, would proceed to wreak havoc behind the lines.

Of course, numbers alone do not pose a threat. It is often asked, and reasonably so, whether the North Korean communists' emphasis on the means of aggression rather than the means of production is not primarily designed to keep the masses in line, and the regime in power. The forces are in uniform, but could Kim Jong-il really send them into battle against the South? After all, the economy is so shattered that there is scarcely fuel for pilots to train. The North has suffered such food shortages in the last 10 years that you'd think that if South Korea reinforced the DMZ with a line of food courts, offering free Big Macs for North Korean customers with rifles, it would all be over in minutes.

I must say, on my first trip to North Korea in 1989, after having lived seven years in Seoul, I was astounded and somewhat angry that such a dump of a place could keep us scared. The "soldiers" I saw were mostly construction workers and farm laborers in uniform. The journey down to Panmunjom from the northern side was a quiet jaunt through the countryside compared to the journey up from the south, which is like the opening scenes of a Spielberg movie. North of Seoul, you go under heavy concrete "tank traps" which would be blown to block the road, past more in the fields — "dragon's teeth," ensuring that invading North Korean tanks would have to make a very wide detour — across a rickety bridge into US 2nd Infantry Division "Warrior Country" which bristles with hardware. Lithe South Koreans and Americans with muscles bulging up their necks on training runs. It's obvious who'd win. So would they ever attack? Although North Korea is the bluffer state, the fact is that we do not know the answer, so we assume "yes" until convinced otherwise.

Here's North Korea's presumed strategy: a massive surprise attack across the DMZ, focusing on South Korean and US military facilities, with special forces creating a movable second front in the South and attacking US bases in Japan and Okinawa. The objective would be to overrun the peninsula with speed and massive destruction before the South could mobilize and before the US could reinforce. North Korea's gamble would be that the United States would be unwilling to accept further casualties to retake the peninsula. This strategy is apparently called, "Occupying South Korea, All the Way to Busan, in Three Days" and was updated after the 1991 Gulf War under Kim Jong-il's direction.[5]

Facing this are South Korea's 560,000 ground forces with 2,250 tanks, 4,850 field artillery pieces, 2,300 armored vehicles, 150 multiple rocket launchers, 30 missiles and 580 helicopters.[6] Navy and marines consist of 67,000 personnel, 200 vessels, and 60 aircraft. The air force numbers 63,000 personnel and 780 aircraft. All men are required to serve in the military for two years and to undergo reserve training and duties for the following eight years. Reservists number around three million.

South Korea's military is arranged in an unusual combined structure alongside US troops. In the event of war, it would effectively fall under the command of an American general. There are just over 37,000 US military personnel in Korea, 27,500 army, 8,300 air force, and around 350 navy personnel and marines. An additional 47,000 American military personnel are located in Japan. The presence is very high profile, with American guards facing the North Koreans in Panmunjom, and manning the forward area of the traditional invasion corridor north of Seoul. Long considered a "tripwire" ensuring US involvement in any repeat of June 1950, these forces are to be redeployed by 2006. For decades, the main US base has been on a swathe of land the size of several golf courses in central Seoul. The US Air Force has over 200 aircraft. In addition, there are some 4,000 US military contractors and 11,500 dependents in South Korea.

As an aside to its defense role, the American presence has a significant impact on the local economy. Apart from the local sourcing of produce and spending by Americans in Korea, the US Department of Defense is one of South Korea's biggest employers.

The combined US-South Korean forces are obviously superior to the North's in technology and have the financial resources for modernization. For this reason, Pyongyang has long stressed its asymmetrical capability: special forces, missiles, and weapons of mass destruction. This capability represents the most serious threat to peace in East Asia.

The nuclear, biological, and chemical component of the North Korean army was formed after the Korean War and is now the centerpiece of its military.[7] North Korea may have as much as

5,000 tons of nerve, blister, and other chemical agents. It may also be able to turn bacteria causing anthrax, smallpox, plague, and cholera into weapons. In the battle strategy outlined above, it is assumed that there would be some chemical strikes against military bases.

The United States estimates that in the late 1980s and early 1990s, North Korea extracted around 13 kilograms of weapons-grade plutonium from its reactor, enough to make up to three Hiroshima-size bombs. Although there are many "ifs" associated with analysis of this secretive development, it is possible that the target was to have between 10 and 20 such weapons by 2000, but that this program was halted in 1994 in a deal with Washington. Under the Agreed Framework, as it was called, the North froze its nuclear program and the US created an international body called the Korea Energy Development Organization (KEDO) to build two light-water reactors and supply 500,000 tons of oil a year for free until construction was complete. South Korea, Japan, and the EU joined the project, the first two paying most of the US$4.6 billion tab. In October 2002, the deal ruptured after Pyongyang was found pursuing a secret uranium-enrichment program. The US halted the oil shipments and Pyongyang retaliated by expelling the international monitors who had been assigned to watch the spent fuel rods as part of the Agreed Framework, withdrawing from the Nuclear Nonproliferation Treaty. The North restarted the reactor, removed the seals on the fuel rods and threatened to extract the plutonium. There was enough there, according to US estimates, for another five or six bombs. By mid-2003, North Korea was saying it had completed this process, although the US and South Korea were unsure if this was a bluff.

North Korea's Nodong missile has a range of 1,300 kilometers and can hit anywhere in South Korea, as well as reach parts of Japan and US bases there. The Taepodong 1 (2,000 kilometers) and 2 (5,000 kilometers) models being worked on at present could cover all of Japan and may soon be able to strike the west coast of the United States. In a highly provocative test in 1998, a Taepodong 1 was fired over Japan. It is believed that the Nodong and Taepodong missiles could deliver nuclear loads, but that at this time of writing the warhead that would allow this has not yet been developed. The weapons would have to be dropped from an aircraft or delivered unconventionally, such as in a cargo container.

As if this weren't enough, Pyongyang has also become a major proliferator. For well over a decade, its missile technology has become a major foreign currency earner. The US has estimated that North Korea earned US$560 million from missile sales to eight countries in 2001. The prospect of Kim Jong-il selling nuclear, biological, or chemical material to terrorists or helping other scruffy states go nuclear earned North Korea its place on President George W. Bush's "Axis of Evil" with Iraq and Iran.

It says something about human nature that, aside from the professionals whose job it is to watch these things, most South Koreans seem unconcerned. In fact, there's a widespread view that the North's nuclear program is not such a bad idea because, they think, Seoul would inherit it upon unification. A sense of false peace seems to prevail.

Despite its proximity, North Korea is distant for South Koreans. They've never been able to drive up and go shopping there. South Korean citizens are not allowed to join tours, which foreign visitors can take, into Panmunjom for fear of incidents. For a long time, they were forbidden from reading North Korean newspapers or watching its TV. Now that they can do these things if they make the effort, they don't want to because what's on offer is so mind-numbingly bad. Although in Washington you get the feeling from time to time that Korea is on the brink, when you're actually in Korea there's so much more to preoccupy citizens than North Korea and its nuclear weapons. Like, corporate governance, the five-day work-week, the stock market, drunk driving, the soaring divorce rate, soaring house prices, soaring use of cosmetics by men, how European beer tastes so much better than the local brew. Is it right that private colleges offer admission for the children of wealthy donors?

North Korea is not high on the list. It's a dull, decrepit embarrassment that has become irrelevant to most South Koreans' lives. They think Kim Jong-il is bluffing and that, frankly, he's giving Koreans a bad name.

Among those who think more about it, you can see the phenomenon, common for a free country when a standoff lasts for a while without much action, of citizens projecting their own decency onto the other side and blaming their own government for the problems. In part, the way South Korean dictators justified denying democracy by referring to the North Korean threat made it hard for democrats to accept the propaganda that North Koreans were dangerous and horrible. The excesses of South Korean propaganda — for example, school students in the 1960s were taught that North Koreans had horns on their heads — contributed to a unification romanticism among some intellectuals, which has abated somewhat with North Korea's continued orneriness in response to the engagement policy begun by former South Korean President Kim Dae-jung.

Many conservatives, on the other hand, blame the mood of false peace on this engagement policy. And, indeed, government authorities in the South have been guilty in recent years of muzzling defectors and security analysts who would speak out on the northern threat for fear that Kim Jong-il would close the whole process down.

But underlying all of the above is another dynamic that South Koreans need to face: the downside of their reliance on America. Although the US presence has deterred the North, it also provided Kim Il-sung with a deluded vision of superiority over South Korea: the limp-wrists in Seoul hide under American skirts, while I forge a new history for all Koreans. His self-reliance philosophy went to the heart of Korea's historical agony. He presented himself as a leader who took on one foreign superpower, the US, while two others, China and the Soviet Union, competed to provide aid. For a people who feel they've been bullied historically, this posture had a profound appeal on both sides of the DMZ, and it was for this reason more than any other that, until South Korea became a democracy, Kim Il-sung's face was not allowed to be shown in South Korea.

In the twenty-first century, South Koreans are no longer tempted by anything that North Korea has to offer. Their approach now is to tread carefully with North Koreans, avoid provoking them and try to gentle them into the modern world through economic exchanges. Given this, the South is unwilling to signal to the North that it is militarily superior. As a result, it is possible that the North may still be under the illusion that it could take on the South Koreans if the Americans were to leave.

South Koreans, meanwhile, feel quite happy to criticize the US troop presence in their country. Anti-Americanism has been very visible since the mid-1980s in South Korea. It festers in the minds of ordinary Koreans and flares up with small incidents, then dies down. In one instance, in late 2002, Koreans took to the streets of Seoul, shredding the Stars and Stripes, to protest a US military tribunal's acquittal of two GIs on negligent homicide charges after their vehicle ran over two girls in what was clearly an accident. Fed in part by disinformation driven through the Internet, the movement swept up ordinary non-political Koreans who otherwise share American values in an emotional wave, which at one point featured nuns innocently wearing "Fucking USA" badges — the title of an anti-American song. Young people mocked the American notion of justice of the "jury of your peers." No wonder the soldiers were let off, went the popular thinking. They were their friends. Cartoons showed Osama bin Laden being tried by a jury of men with beards. This took place in the lead up to the December 2002 presidential election. As indication of how widespread was the sentiment, the conservative candidate, Lee Hoi-chang, signed a petition calling for a rewrite of the Status of Forces Agreement, the legal arrangement under which US forces serve in Korea, and took a photo op with the parents of the two girls. (His liberal opponent and the eventual winner, Roh Moo-hyun, who had more support from the anti-American activists, declined, saying it was "inappropriate.")

When American columnists started suggesting that perhaps the troops should be withdrawn if they were not wanted, activists found a new charge to levy at the Americans: that of failing to understand their anti-Americanism. What we're really saying, the activists said, is that an overwhelming majority of Koreans want the US relationship and want the troops. It's just that they don't like the American "attitude." Americans should not look down on Koreans.

Actually, you've got to have some sympathy for the Koreans. They've suffered from leadership failure on this issue. Under Syngman Rhee and Park Chung-hee, they were told that Americans were on their soil to protect them (i.e. for Korean national interests). When the US failed to prevent the 1980 takeover of General Chun Doo-hwan, this rather limited perception began to change. Many wrongly assumed that this dictator, who sent murderous special forces against student demonstrators, came to power with US backing, a perception that Chun himself encouraged. In the 1980s, many intellectuals became convinced that US troops were in Korea to protect only American interests. In other words, US forces have a huge base in downtown Seoul because they insist on it and there's nothing we poor Koreans can do about it. This viewpoint has gained wide acceptance among the general populace because political leaders have lacked the courage to stand up at such times and point out that the two countries have converging national interests and that both are being served by US forces in Korea.

They fail to do so because they recognize anti-US outbursts for what they are — emotion — and feel it wiser for their political careers to keep their heads down and let them blow over.

The process by which the 2002 wave dissipated is instructive. One night in early January 2003, an official at the Ministry of Finance and Economy received a call from Moody's in New York. The ratings agency was to hold a meeting to discuss South Korea's sovereign rating and wanted to advise the official that it was likely to be downgraded. Three were factors influencing investors: the North Korea nuclear issue, anti-Americanism, and the fact that the president-elect, Roh Moo-hyun, was being portrayed by the US media as pro-labor and anti-American. The official asked Moody's to visit and meet Roh's transition team before making their judgment. He then called the Blue House, which advised Roh and the economic officials in the transition team to take action. Within a few days, Roh decided on a first-ever visit to the United States, visited with the commander of US Forces Korea, addressed a joint meeting of the American and European Chambers of Commerce in Seoul, gave interviews to CNN and *The New York Times*, and publicly called on activists to end the anti-US protests, which they did.[8]

One of the frustrations for South Korean officials regarding the nuclear threat from North Korea is, of course, that this is one security problem that they are not in a good position to solve. Not only do the Americans have the power to address it, but also the North Koreans refuse to talk to South Korea about it. They insist that they will only talk to the Americans.

In figuring out North Korean intentions, all eyes are on Kim Jong-il. His is the finger on the button. He is the all-powerful chairman of the National Defense Commission and commander-in-chief. He lacks revolutionary credentials and military experience, and couldn't drop and give you ten if his life depended on it, but has made up for this by creating loyalty among the few top brass and keeping them wedded to their privileges.

This feat was achieved first by the support of Jong-il's father, who made him a marshal. Since Kim Il-sung's death, the Dear Leader has promoted an unprecedented number of generals. During the famines of the later 1990s, the army received preferential treatment, a blessing in disguise for men on military service. He has introduced a "Military First" — i.e. "Party Second" — policy which is especially apparent in Pyongyang. One visitor in early 2003 said that the Sunday sermon at one of the country's two Protestant churches (which, along with the single Catholic church, are propaganda creations) was about how God supports the policy. The army is the country's biggest corporation, a mini-state within a state. It has its own mines, factories, and trading companies in what is known officially as the Second Economy. Without it, Kim Jong-il would have been fired for incompetence by now.

4

Dear Boy

Kim Jong-il is North Korea's second leader since its founding in 1946. Despite his long grooming for the position, despite having day-to-day run the country as his father aged, despite his actual leadership since his father's death, and despite the shelves of biographies and daily column inches devoted to him each day in the North Korean media, he remains something of a mystery.

If North Korea is an intelligence black hole, then that invisible part of Kim Jong-il — his thoughts, impulses and intentions — are the heart of the darkness.

Would this man with his finger on the nuclear button press it? Will the world yet see the use of nuclear weapons before they are eventually turned into ploughshares and will they be North Korean? Just who is this man who gives new meaning to the term "bad hair day"? We don't know.

Vacuums of knowledge tend to suck in interpretations that tell as much about their source as about their object. Thus, for a long time, South Korean intelligence authorities portrayed him as a dangerous lunatic. He was known to be a playboy, the world's biggest single purchaser of Hennessy's pricey Paradis brand of cognac. He was bad tempered. He surrounded himself with pretty girls. He had a huge collection of western movies and probably porn. He had been behind commando attacks on South Korean targets. But when, in June 2000, he turned out unexpectedly on the tarmac at Pyongyang's Sunan Airport to greet South Korean President Kim Dae-jung on his historic visit to the North, southerners went all warm and fuzzy. It was a memorable day. That morning, I'd had an operation to surgically enlarge my nasal passages. I watched the two leaders meet on TV with two tampon-like things inserted bloodily into my nose. The women in the North Korean rent-a-crowd waved and jigged up and down with excitement, more at catching a glimpse of Kim Jong-Elvis than at the momentousness of the occasion. Kim Dae-jung walked with a Charlie Chaplin waddle, the result of injuries from an auto accident he believes was an assassination attempt by dictator Park Chung-hee. Kim Jong-il slowed down, in polite deference to his elder counterpart. This touched South Korean viewers, who reminded themselves that half their friends fit that bad-tempered playboy description. They started referring to him politely by his title, "Chairman Kim." Polls showed that expectations of a North Korean invasion dropped from 40 to 10 percent.

Such rapidly shifting perceptions underscore South Korean yearning for reconciliation and an end to fear. But they do little to help us figure the man. North Korean sources don't help much either. There, the masses are bombarded with propaganda. They have no idea, for example, that Chairman Kim is fussy about how his *pelmeni* dumplings are cooked.[1] He doesn't give fireside chats or get interviewed by North Korean Ted Koppels. He deals with local reporters, but this is more by way of loving, fatherly guidance to fellow travelers than answering searching questions like, "In our country's official name, the Democratic People's Republic of Korea, what does 'Democratic' mean?"

Talking of which, while the world thinks that the Pentagon invented the concept of the "embedded" reporter in the 2003 Iraq War, it might come as a surprise to learn that North Korea pioneered this democratic concept a long time ago. For many years, journalists from the *Rodong Shinmun* and other leading organs were embedded with the late Great Leader Kim Il-sung as he toured the country giving his famous "on-the-spot guidance," without which, we must admit, North Korea might have become a more developed country. Many of their stories are to be found in a 1983 North Korean publication called *The Great Teacher of Journalists: Kim Jong-il* — long a bestseller among the half-dozen western reporters to get visas each year (but later published in the Netherlands and made available to the galaxy on amazon.com). This is one of those works which you can open at any page at random and find deep truth. Let's share.

One day in 1963, the book says, the Great Leader Kim Il-sung was scheduled to climb Mt. Paekdu, on the Chinese border, to give some on-the-spot guidance about something.[2] The embedded journalists were in tow. As they were about to set off up the mountain, the reporters bumped into 21-year-old Kim Jong-il.[3]

"Have you had breakfast?" he asked solicitously. They told him that the kitchen had prepared rice and side dishes, but as the soup wasn't ready, they were not able to eat. They said they'd wait until they'd returned from Mt. Paekdu. Sensing their frustration, young Kim Jong-il said with a kind smile: "Today is a memorable day when the Great Leader will climb Mt. Paekdu. So you must make full preparations for collecting information. If you start right now, you may miss a meal. I can't allow you to start without having your breakfast. You have no time. So, you should go to the dining room and take that which is ready."

This simple suggestion cut through canteen red tape. But it also perplexed the reporters because they weren't sure, as Koreans, whether it's actually possible to eat a meal without soup. What Kim Jong-il did next was incredible. He himself walked into the dining room and proposed they all start tucking in together.

"Comrade journalists, there is no need to stand on ceremony. Now, come nearer and sit down," he said. And, according to the book, he "himself led them by the hand to seat them at the table."

Needless to say, the stories that day were positive.

A possible explanation for Kim Jong-il's youthful bonding with hacks is that he can relate to their struggle.

"I myself have written a great deal," he is quoted as saying, "and from my own experience I know that writing is most difficult. Therefore, those who treat, assign and write articles can be called heroes." Accordingly, he has awarded deserving editors and reporters with awards such as People's Journalist, Merited Journalist, Labor Hero, and the highest honor of all, the Kim Il-sung Prize. (You have to ask, did anyone think to honor the embedded reporters in Iraq this way? No, all they got was free C rations.)

Despite the quality time he has spent with local reporters, Kim Jong-il doesn't meet the foreign press. The only interview he's ever given to a US reporter was a six-hour session in 2000 with Moon Myong-ja, of the Washington-based *U.S.-Asian News Service.* In the same year, he had a lunch session with South Korean publishers.[4] The big boys from muscular publications like *The New York Times* and *The Washington Post* would scratch each other's eyes out to claim the "first-ever western interview." (I personally feel these newspapers are unreasonably dominant and would like to see the *National Enquirer* given a chance to contribute to the debate on North Korea.) On the broadcast side, CNN has reported from North Korea and would be an obvious choice for Kim Jong-il's first interview. But Kim Jong-il likes to surprise and may have at one point considered a different type of TV debut. At the end of a visit to North Korea in 1992, the editor of *The Washington Times*, Wesley Pruden, in final remarks of thanks in the VIP lounge of the airport, told officials that their country reminded him of "an American TV program called 'Mister Rogers' Neighborhood'." They took notes. (No doubt they later learned that the last original program was taped in 2001 and that Fred Rogers died in 2003.)

Although Kim Jong-il was second-top story in North Korea for decades, the masses didn't even hear his voice until 1992 when he did spake unto them on Armed Forces Day, saying, "Glory to the people's heroic military!" This helped dispel my personal suspicion that the coyness was actually because he was vocally challenged (maybe he sounded as if he was on helium or something). But, that aside, his one-line declaration revealed as little about him as if he'd declared, "I declare these Olympics open," a declaration he probably fantasizes about making.

In any attempt to analyze Kim Jong-il, we should start by stating the obvious: that both his personal and political character can only be understood with reference to the overwhelming presence of his father, Kim Il-sung, throughout his life. That, plus the fact that he's a wee fellow — just five feet two inches — with a boyish hairdo, always reminds me of a song by The Who:

> I'm a substitute for another guy
> I look pretty tall but my heels are high
> Simple things seem so complicated
> I look pretty young, but I'm just backdated — Yeah

In July 1968, the Dear Substitute was walking with some of his father's guerilla veterans on Mt. Paekdu.

"When I come to Mt. Paekdu through the thick forests, I feel I have passed through the gate and am standing in the courtyard of my home," he told them.[5] As a boy, he went on, he once asked his mother, Kim Jong-suk, where he was from.

"Your home is Mt. Paekdu, the highest mountain of Korea," she said. "There is Lake Chon on Mt. Paekdu, and there are a lot of trees there. It is where your father defeated the Japanese army. Go to Mt. Paekdu when you are older." This was a very nice thing to say to a little boy. The still lake in the crater of the mountain is associated with the country's mythical founding. It was her way of saying, "You're special."

From this recollection, true or false, official North Korean accounts segue into the claim that Jong-il entered the world in a secret guerilla camp there on February 16, 1942. In a 1999 interview with the left-tilting South Korean daily *Hankyoreh Shinmun* that appears to support this history, one of his mother's comrades, Lee Min, said that Kim Jong-suk and other women fighters snuck into the secret camp on the Paekdu mountain in the summer of 1941 and that Kim Jong-il was born there. According to Lee, news of the birth of his first child reached Kim Il-sung by radio at the army camp in Vyatskoye, near Khabarovsk in the former Soviet Union, where he was based. Mother and child did not return to Vyatskoye till the following year, Lee said.[6] However, in a meeting a few weeks after the *Hankyoreh* interview later with the writer Peter Hyun, Lee declined to talk about the whereabouts of Kim Jong-il's birthplace. Hyun took this reticence to mean that the earlier *Hankyoreh* interview may have contained mistruths that she chose not to repeat.[7] Indeed, most foreign sources believe that Kim Jong-il was actually born in the army camp in Vyatskoye.

Either way, Paekdu makes for a better story. The hagiography brigade has done a cracking job.

> The log cabin at the camp and the tall trees around it were covered with snow... All the guerrillas at the camp exchanged the news of the birth of a baby to their leader. As if by mutual consent, they gathered around the flag which was fluttering in the morning sun, celebrated the birth of Kim Jong Il and pledged to fight for an early liberation of their fatherland.[8]

As I've suggested, it is possible that this story is a fib, awareness of which would not especially disturb the propagandist's conscience. For Marxist-Leninists, making up stuff in the service of a greater truth — their political power — amounts to truth.

The date is questioned, too. Some analysts have claimed that the Dear Substitute was born in 1941, but changed the year to get into better rhythm with his father (who was born in 1912).[9] The suspicion is that Kim Jong-il figured that celebrating his fiftieth, for example, and his dad's eightieth within a few weeks would make for a better party. I wonder, though, if this is not a misinterpretation. Knowing that Kim Jong-il took care not to upstage his father, perhaps he wanted to avoid celebrating a meaningful birthday, like, say, his fortieth, in the year that his father would have been a less meaningful 71-year-old? Who knows? I should point out, though, that doctoring records is much less of a crime for Koreans of that era than it is for Americans. For example, former South Korean President and 2000 Nobel Peace Prize winner Kim Dae-jung is actually almost two years older than his official age, having adjusted his birthday to avoid Japanese military service.

On a similar note, it is common for Koreans to alter their names in a bid to improve their fortunes. According to the Chinese character for *Jong* and *Il*, Kim Jong-il's name meant "righteous the first." But *Il* can also mean "sun," as in Kim Il-sung's name. Jong-il changed to this meaning around 1980, thus making his name "Righteous Sun." After her death, the "Jong" in his mother Kim Jong-suk's name was changed from its original meaning of "virtue" to "righteousness."[10] In this way, Kim Jong-il sought to draw on his parents' fortune.

Jong-il apparently took after his mother. Kim Jong-suk was a short woman with attractively long eyelashes and her skin was darkened by exposure to the sun.[11] "She was quick, generous and had many talents," Lee Min remembers. Men and women lived separately and, for three years, the two women shared the same quarters in the camp. "She was a good cook, good needle worker, good dancer, good actress, good singer and so on." Interestingly,

"Kim Il-sung was a good drama director and writer, and Kim Jong-suk was good at directing dancing and often danced herself."

In his memoirs, Kim Il-sung described his wife as a very sacrificial and devoted colleague and a considerate woman, whose actions in engaging the enemy saved his life more than once.[12] One winter, he was told that she had washed his clothes and was wearing them herself so they would dry. He called her in to reprimand her. "I was near tears when I saw her face so pale from the cold," he wrote. "To think that she had done for me what my mother dared not do in her lifetime, I did not know what to say to her." She also cut her hair to line his shoes. Despite this, there was a certain formality in their relationship. The Great Leader said that she always called him "General" or later, "Comrade Premier."

Apparently, Jong-suk was not able to produce enough milk to feed the Dear Baby and so asked another nursing mother, Yi Jae-dok, to breast-feed him.[13] It is said that, as his mother had guerrilla duties, she often handed him over to the care of other women in the camp.

Jong-il went by the Russian nickname "Yura" even after returning to Korea. He had a younger brother, Man-il, whose nickname was "Shura," and a sister, Kyung-hee. In her interview with Peter Hyun, Lee Min recalls Jong-il as a young boy:

> Kim Jong-il was a bright and agile child. He had his mother's dark black eyes and dark complexion. He was a cute boy. After kindergarten, there was no one to look after him and so Kim Jong-suk brought him to our training camp with her. Kim Jong-il carried a wooden rifle and marched alongside the fighters in training. In 1945, liberation came and [my Chinese husband and I] left for Manchuria in September of that year. I recall that Kim Jong-suk stayed at the camp a little bit longer and left in

November. By that time, she had [had] her second son. He was about two years younger than Jong-il.

Chen and I went to see Kim Il-sung before we left the camp. They came out and embraced us. Kim Jong-il insisted on going with us and his mother had to do some spanking.

Kim Jong-il played with a wooden rifle. When he played with... other kids, Jong-il had to be the commander... I would ask him if he could kill the Japanese with a wooden gun. He would reply confidently that he could. I would tell him that he needed a real gun to kill a Japanese and then he would ask his mother for a real gun. Kim Jong-suk told him: 'No, you cannot have Dad's gun. You must use your wooden gun to take a real gun from the enemy. That's the only way you would become a general like your Dad.' Kim Jong-suk was quite strict with Jong-il but I never saw her hit him.[14]

Sometimes the soldiers would take Yura to the Amur River to show him the boats and migrating birds.[15] His father wrote that Yura "had an unusual start to life, as born to guerrillas, he grew up in clothes impregnated with powder smoke, eating army rations and hearing shouts of military command... He was precocious, probably because he grew up under the influence of the guerrillas. Their noble feelings and emotions became rich nourishment for his mind and their mettle, as soaring as the peak of Mt. Paekdu, added flesh and blood to his manly personality." (The memoirs were ghost-written, in case you're thinking the Great Leader is getting carried away here.)

In 1947, when Jong-il was five, and the family was living in the official residence of the prime minister in Pyongyang, three-year-old Shura fell into the pond in the back garden and drowned. By some accounts, the two were playing together at the time. One North Korean defector has suggested that Jong-il pushed him in and laughed as his brother struggled and drowned, but doesn't reveal how he came by this explosive information.[16] As much as one would like to draw a straight line from this incident to Kim Jong-il the horned, cloven-hoofed leader, the truth is that we have no idea what happened, let alone how he experienced it, whether he was responsible, felt responsible or was made to feel responsible. We may assume, though, that this family tragedy is associated with his earliest memories.

In September 1949, when Kim Jong-il was seven and attending the kindergarten of Namsan Elementary School in Pyongyang, his mother died of complications from an ectopic pregnancy. Shura's death is ignored in North Korean accounts. (It's possible no propagandist dared upset anyone by asking for the information). However, the death of Kim Jong-il's mother is milked for every tear to strengthen the emotional bond between weepy subject and suffering leader. According to one account, Kim Jong-suk's coffin was in the Central Committee building. When father and son went to pay their respects, Kim Il-sung asked for the gold watch that he'd given to her as a retroactive wedding present and instructed that she be buried with it.

> A woman fighter put the watch on the wrist of the deceased. On seeing this, [Kim Jong-il] put his face to his mother's breast and wept. The women fighters picked up the boy to take him away from the side of his mother, whereupon the father leader said in a hoarse voice, "Leave him alone. Tomorrow he will have no mother any more in whose embrace to cry.[17]

When the hearse moved off, according to this biography of Kim Jong-il, a relative had to hold him back.

Accounts differ on what happened to Jong-il and his sister at this point. After his mother's death, it is believed that they were first looked after by Kim Il-sung's aide de camp, Lee Ul-sol, and then by partisan comrade Kim Ok-sun, the wife of Kim Il-sung's former chief-of-staff, Choe Kwang. It is indicative of Kim Il-sung's confidence at the start of the Korean War in June 1950, that he did not evacuate his children. (When the tide turned against the North in the war, the two siblings were evacuated to Jilin in China).

The biography quoted above describes the eight year-old boy's war experience. This part is almost certainly apocryphal, but is worth quoting at length because it's an illustration of how hatred is taught in North Korea.

Whenever enemy planes appeared, the young dear leader would rush up to the top of the hill in front of his house and look down indignantly on the terrible scene of Pyongyang being bombed.

He was an eyewitness of the saturation bombing of Pyongyang in which the heinous American imperialist murderers destroyed factories, schools, theatres and houses viciously at random, revealing their true nature as beasts. Every time he was watching streets being reduced to heaps of ashes and the blood of innocent people spilt, he made up his mind, trembling all over with indignation:

"You foes, I will grow up to be an avenger and make you pay a thousand times more for the blood shed by our people!"

One day, he had an opportunity of seeing with his own eyes an American imperialist marauder who had burned down the dear city and had been cruelly killing the Korean people. That day an airman of the enemy plane hit by the People's Army anti-aircraft fire over Pyongyang parachuted down into a ravine some [distance] from his home. The dear leader wanted to take a good look at the brute who alighted with a parachute to save his own life after heartlessly murdering a countless number of the Korean people.

So he rushed to the scene at the head of other schoolchildren. He arrived at the place when the People's Army men had just captured the enemy flier. The fellow was goggling his deep-set cunning eyes, trembling with fear. He looked like a cornered wolf.

This was the first time for the dear leader to stand face to face with one of the US imperialists, the sworn enemy of the Korean people for more than a hundred years, who had pounced on them again to enslave them. On seeing the villain, the schoolchildren picked up pebbles and closed in on him threateningly, unable to restrain their rising indignation.

At this moment the dear leader who had been glaring fiercely at the enemy flier with piercing eyes took a step forward before the schoolchildren. "Look at that fellow, how frightened he is and what a poor figure he is cutting. No matter how many packs of those brutes may attack us, we need not fear them. We should beat the wolves mercilessly with a stick.[18]

Interestingly, in the same book, the author claims that father and son narrowly escaped when US warplanes bombed a road shortly after their car had turned off it. Again, while we may assume such facts are massaged, this scene provides a special insight into North Korean acceptance of elite rudeness. A guard standing at a fork in the main road was waving the car in the direction that was shortly bombed, but Kim Il-sung wanted to go on the road less traveled.[19] "General, the lane is very rough," the nameless near-hero of Korean history said. "And there are no guards posted along it." Kim Il-sung repeated his request, and the guard stood there not quite knowing what to do. At this point, Kim Jong-il, who would have been around eight or nine years old, intervened. "Why are you standing like that? Didn't the General say the car should go along the lane? Let the car go the way requested by the General." You wonder if North Korean readers, reading this, are impressed by the Dear Leader's leaderly qualities, and by his loyalty to the Great Leader, or, whether, reading between the lines, they think he was a brat.

By all accounts he was.

In biographies of Korean male achievers, there are a few key themes: worthy ancestors whose deeds somehow presage the birth of the hero, a long-suffering mother and an absent father, off fighting for a noble cause. Also helpful, but not essential, is a tendency to embarrass teachers with youthful wisdom. Jong-il had this one in buckets. Even in kindergarten, fawners say, his questions would befuddle teachers. Why are some flowers red and others yellow? Why is the moon sometimes full? How do fish breathe?[20] No wonder he doesn't want to be interviewed by American reporters. He'd get what he's been giving all his life. Do you color your hair? How do you see North Korea's image overseas? Do you think diplomats should raise money by selling drugs?

Kim Jong-il appears to have been rather wild in a way that typifies elite children in both Koreas, where parents may demand obedience to themselves but do not teach their children to respect social inferiors. I met one such member of the elite in Pyongyang who told me he had once punched his professor at university. This young man talked in ways that would have got other people sent to the gulag. We may safely assume that it must have been difficult for guardians and teachers to tell the son of Kim Il-sung what to do. Such a lack of disciplining would have made it difficult for Kim Jong-il to learn self-discipline, as later stories of his bad temper would seem to bear out.

He certainly was shunted from one school to another. In 1952, back in Pyongyang, Kim Jong-il entered the Man-gyong-dae Revolutionary School. The next year he was moved to another school before being admitted as a fifth grader into the No. 4 Pyongyang Elementary School.

At the Man-gyong-dae school, Kim Jong-il allegedly excelled at math, among other things. The first time the students did sums with three-figure numbers, the teacher asked them to do it in their heads. Guess who was the only one with the correct answer? "All the children looked up at the dear leader with eyes full of joy and admiration. What a splendid mathematical gift he has possessed, they thought."[21] It was natural that when he grew up, he would be the one chosen to lead the North Korean economy.

In a report for her successor, the Dear Leader's teacher offers some advice for tiptoeing around the precocious child. The teacher is not named and there is no indication how the biographer quoting her obtained the material. It may be an invention, but as an official portrayal of the young Jong-il, it's hard to resist.

1. The teacher should study without delay and in detail the works, especially the latest works, of General Kim Il Sung, reports of the Supreme Headquarters, the situation in and out of the country, etc.

   These are what Kim Jong Il is most concerned about, and he inquires about them at any moment. He has a considerable knowledge about them, so the teacher should never answer his questions without reading, hearing and studying.

   * *Without being fully prepared the teacher may find himself in an awkward situation not knowing what to answer to his questions.*

2. Kim Jong Il loathes one who breaks one's promises. Therefore, if the teacher neglects or breaks his promises, he will forfeit his authority as a teacher.

3. Kim Jong Il treasures time very much. The daily schedule should be laid out meticulously so that there may be no time spent idly and he should be guided to observe it strictly. His

temperament is like the current of a swift river, so he does not know standstill and stagnation but always makes progress.

4. Kim Jong Il is of such a character that he carries everything through to the end. Once he has started a thing, he will never give it up halfway however difficult it may be. Even without the help of the teacher he will bring it to completion by all means.

5. Kim Jong Il has an extraordinary spirit of inquiry. When the teacher puts a question, he will delve into it and solve it at all costs. Not satisfied with this, he will study it to a greater extent.

   So the teacher must know the answer to the question and, further, have a thorough knowledge of how the answer (or conclusion) is derived.

6. Kim Jong Il does not want and even detests special favours. So the teacher must be careful about this. He would rather like the teacher to be more exacting towards him. Therefore, the teacher should treat him equally with other pupils while being strict in making demands.

   For instance, when checking on his homework notebook or grading his examination papers, the teacher should be strict and appraise the results as they are shown. Sometimes, it is necessary to evaluate them even more strictly.

7. Kim Jong Il greatly hates lagging behind others. In this light, if the teacher becomes his rival and helps to develop his thinking faculty continuously, this will be very effective.

8. Kim Jong Il has an uncommon zeal for work. When he is given many assignments, he is very much pleased, but when a small or no assignment whatsoever is given, he becomes reticent and depressed.

   * *This must always be taken into consideration.*

9. Kim Jong Il is psychologically more precocious than other pupils, very sensitive and magnanimous and has a great thinking power. So he will be bored when explanations are too lengthy or repeated during the lessons.
   This must be taken into consideration in preparing the programme of instruction.

10. Kim Jong Il keeps himself neat and trim and is exceptionally well-mannered.
    The teacher must take great care to foster and develop his good qualities and educate all other pupils to follow his example.

11. The favorite dishes of Kim Jong Il are: in winter, rich bean-paste soup; in spring, seasoned crowndaisy or other spring-greens; in summer, cold cucumber soup or rice hash; in autumn, rice wrapped in leaves of celery cabbage or coarse bean-curd.
    He likes dining together with other pupils.

12. The teacher should always watch the eyes of Kim Jong Il. When he looks straight at the teacher, the latter can be assured that he is speaking or acting correctly, but when he looks away or shows aloofness from the teacher, the latter should known that his own speech or act is at fault and should correct it promptly. In other words, it will be proper to regard the eyes of Kim Jong Il as an indicator of right and wrong.[22]

Reading through these closely, you wonder if the teacher whispered to her successor, "Ignore the even points, focus on the odd ones."

In his interview with Moon Myong-ja in 2000, Kim Jong-il said that a "leader must labor together with the people."[23] Such "laboring with the people" is integral to North Korean education and Jong-il had his share of it. In 1958, while a student at

Namsan Senior High School, he visited several construction sites and factories, including the Pyongyang Rubber Factory, the Pyongyang Cornstarch Factory, the Pyongyang Textile Mill, and the Hwanghae Iron Works. For six weeks in May and June that year, he worked with other members of the Democratic Youth League at a construction facility making concrete sections for prefabricated buildings.

He graduated from high school in 1960.

In September 1960, he enrolled at Kim Il Sung University, the country's top college, to study political economy. There he allegedly prompted a movement among students to read 10,000 words of Kim Il-sung's works a year.[24] He reportedly had a special tutor for every subject, assigned by his cousin, Kim Shin-sook, who was tasked with managing his college education.[25]

In the following year, he worked with other students on road construction in Pyongyang. Part of his curriculum included practical experience in the Pyongyang Textile Machinery Factory. There, too, his genius was in evidence. In a chapter entitled, "A Girl Machine Operator Stirred to Excitement" from the biography *Kim Jong Il: The People's Leader*, there is a suggestive account of how he taught a "young and agile" worker how to properly "oil her machine."[26] As she had finished before him, he went to admire her oiled and polished lathe. He tried to turn the handle of the vice. (For better effect, you might want to read the next section out loud.)

> "How stiff! What's the matter?" he asked the girl.
>
> "It has always been so," was her answer.
>
> "It can't be. It can't be stiff if it is oiled. When was it oiled?"
>
> "The handle of the vice has no oilhole," the girl answered definitely.
>
> "No hole? How many oilholes has this machine in all?"

"Twenty-one."

[At this, Kim Jong-il takes a look and scrapes away some dirt, revealing a small hole.]

The girl blushed, ashamed of her ignorance of the principle of [mechanics] and of the number of oilholes in her own machine which she had handled as carefully as her own flesh.

Seeing her embarrassment, he said, "It is fortunate that we have found the oilhole before it is too late." And he oiled the hole in person, and then told the girl to have a try at the handle.

The handle worked so smoothly that it seemed to turn round by itself.

The young girl clapped her hands with delight as if she had found something mysterious.

And thus, I'll be bound, began his lifelong quest for oilholes. In the summer of 1962, the Dear Oiler went to Changsong and Sakju counties in the north of the country by the Yalu River to research local industry and living conditions. His analysis was allegedly used as the basis for measures introduced by Kim Il-sung later that year to develop the local economy there. From this material, he is said to have developed his graduating thesis on "The Position and Role of the Country in Socialist Construction."

He graduated from university in May 1964.

CHAPTER
5

Dear Successor

B y the custom of the day, Kim Il-sung was old to be having his first child at 30. Boys were usually married in their teens and usually to older girls. Had he not been a guerrilla of no fixed abode, he might have had four or five children by then and more on the way. It would not be unreasonable to assume the Great Leader had previous love interests.

Indeed, one book by a former Soviet-Korean communist claims that Jong-il's mother, Kim Jong-suk, was not the Great Leader's first wife. That distinction allegedly went to Han Seong-hee, who was head of the partisan women's department.[1] She is said to have been caught and jailed by the Japanese authorities in 1940. One reason her story may have become obscured was that she changed her name twice. She told the Japanese interrogators her name was Kim Hye-sun. An uncle helped obtain her release on condition that she sever ties with the revolutionaries. By the time of Korea's liberation from Japanese rule, she was going under the name Han Yong-suk, was remarried and had had four children. Apparently, Kim Il-sung tracked her down, although it is not known if they met. She rose to become a Party county chief, but was later purged, allegedly for expressing her disapproval of the Great Leader's rumored plans

63

to marry a secretary after Kim Jong-il's mother had died. In the mid-1950s, she was demoted to factory work. Her fate thereafter is unknown.

Kim Jong-il may even today be unaware of this rumored relationship. It's hard to imagine anyone bringing it up with him.

For probably as long as the Dear Leader could remember, however, the main relationship in his father's life was with a woman called Kim Song-ae. The two are believed to have married in 1951, when Kim Jong-il was nine, but it is possible they were together before Jong-suk's death.[2] Very little has ever been made public about Kim Song-ae, but she is said to have been the secretary to the security guard at his residence.[3] The marriage was publicly announced in 1963 and she emerged in 1965 as the vice-chair of the Democratic Women's Union. Later, she was appointed to the Central Committee of the Workers' Party and the Standing Committee of the Supreme People's Assembly, the North Korean parliament. Their first child, a boy, Kim Pyong-il, was born in 1954. They went on to have one more boy, Yong-il, and a girl, Kyung-jin.

After the war, Kim Jong-il grew to adolescence in this blended family. Quite naturally, he is said to have struggled with his father's remarriage. Judging by the lower profile his stepmother has adopted since Kim Il-sung's death in 1994, we may assume tensions with Jong-il that were never resolved.

This family environment complicates the question of how Kim Jong-il came to be selected as the next in line to the dictator's throne. No one in the family would have been backing him. The stage was better set for his half-brother Pyong-il to be seen as the new "first son," and for Jong-il to be the more obscure Billy Carter/Roger Clinton figure identified in the pictures as "second left, back row, with the hair." Such speculation was indeed fueled in the 1990s — mostly overseas, where it didn't matter — because people were impressed with the suave, English-speaking Pyong-il, a diplomat (he is the ambassador to

Poland at the time of writing), a dead ringer for his father, minus the goiter, and said to be popular with the military because he'd actually served in it.

We should remember, however, that Kim Il-sung and his cohorts were communists, and communists didn't go for the idea of hereditary succession. In fact, they considered it "originally a product of slave societies... later adopted by feudal lords as a means to perpetuate dictatorial rule." At least that's what the 1970 edition of Pyongyang's *Dictionary of Political Terminologies* had to say.[4]

What changed?

There are two schools of thought and neither really fits the broad assumption that Kim Il-sung couldn't shake off a feudal Confucian mindset and insisted on establishing a dynasty. The first is that the idea came from the partisans. The second is that Kim Jong-il himself manipulated the partisans and executed a very skillful, long-term power play.

Taking the first, it's possible that the idea of Kim Jong-il as successor grew out of a chance meeting in Moscow's Red Square between Vyacheslav Molotov, Stalin's foreign minister, and Lim Chun-chu, one of Kim Il-sung's partisans and a diplomat, some time in the 1960s. By that time, Molotov had been expelled from the Communist Party for criticizing then Soviet leader Nikita Kruschchev. Molotov advised Lim, an intellectual who was writing up the partisans' history, to be mindful of the Soviet experience. Lim came to believe that if the successor were not loyal to the leader, the revolution and the Party would eventually collapse. The reason we should give weight to this episode is that Kim Il-sung cites it in the section of his memoirs about the succession.[5] Kim Il-sung believed that the Soviet Union had grown rapidly into a world power because Lenin chose a good successor, and that "things began to go astray" after Krushchev came to power and vilified Stalin. From this line of reasoning, it was but a short step back into Korean tradition to propose the prince.

At this time, Pyong-il was only in his early teens. What's more, his mother had not been a partisan. Kim Jong-il, on the other hand, had the perfect heritage, as far as the guerrilla generation was concerned. But was he up to the job?

Jong-il was known to be wild and bolshie with authority, a stroppy kid like Dr Evil's son in the *Austin Powers* movies. But, we should note, the key qualification was loyalty to the Great Leader. Kim Jong-il had been working, since graduating from college, in the Party Central Committee's Department of Organization and Guidance. At one point, in 1967, there was a purge of some "vacillating elements influenced by external factionalism and opportunism" in the Party.[6] To underscore his loyalty, Kim Jong-il was later credited with having exposed the plot that led to the purge. It is also possible that his uncle Yong-ju, who headed the department and who also had ambitions to be the successor, used the purges to try and advance himself.

Kim Jong-il was also at this time fascinated by the movie industry. This risked appearing flaky, but he, in fact, showed his loyalty here, too. Among his speeches were one entitled, "Let's Produce More Revolutionary Films Reflecting the Socialist Reality!" and another, "For a New Upsurge in Film Production."

Whatever else Jong-il did in his late twenties, he impressed the veterans around Kim Il-sung. It is possible that they persuaded Kim Il-sung that he was the man. The official version is that, at first, the Great Leader rejected the idea.[7] However, by some time in the late 1960s, he was on board. That bit about hereditary succession being a bad idea had been edited out by the time the 1972 edition of the dictionary hit the shelves.

Although chosen, there was no formal announcement for several years.

Kim Jong-il is not known to have been especially bloodthirsty in his quest for power, yet two unconfirmed incidents mentioned by his nephew Lee Han-yong, who defected to South Korea in 1982 (and who was murdered in Seoul in 1997 by an unknown assailant), suggest a certain ruthlessness.[8] In one case, in the early 1970s, according to Lee, a Party official rather flatteringly suggested that Kim Jong-il should be officially declared the successor. Apparently, Jong-il's response was to shoot him. The crime? Challenging Kim Il-sung. In other words, it was Kim Il-sung's place, and Kim Il-sung's only, to make such comments. Jong-il did not want this type of talk emanating from the people around him, lest it create the impression that he was engineering his ascension.

We do not have confirmation of this incident from other sources, but Lee's explanation suggests that Kim Jong-il was shrewdly aware that his position was not completely secure. During this period, Kim Jong-il had to work hard to maintain his father's continued support. Indeed, had he made serious errors over the 20 or so years before he actually assumed power or if, in particular, he had suggested that he might take the country in a different direction from his father, he would have been passed over.

The second incident some years later involved secret parties that Jong-il used to throw for his intimates. It was this weakness for partying that, above all, he wished to keep from his rather austere father. One fellow party animal, named Lee Myong-jae, reportedly went home completely legless and babbled in his sleep. His wife wrote a letter to Kim Il-sung asking him to reprimand her husband for drinking so much. The letter was intercepted by Kim Jong-il, who scolded Lee. Lee's response was to request Kim Jong-il's permission to execute his wife himself. It was granted.

Hwang Jang-yop, the North Korean academic who developed the country's governing *Juche* philosophy and later defected to South Korea, has suggested that Kim Jong-il manipulated his father from the start. "He was jealous and cunning," Hwang writes. "I could see that he craved power."[9]

This may be the case, but we should also note that Hwang has a strong dislike of Kim Jong-il and may be overstating the degree of manipulation. My own sense over the years has been that the driving force behind the creation of the world's first communist dynasty was the effort by a son to maintain his father's affection and support. This is also my read on the evidence presented by Hwang. The former dean of Kim Il-sung University, Hwang first met Kim Jong-il in January 1959, when they both accompanied Kim Il-sung on a trip to Moscow.

> Knowing I was a professor at Kim Il-sung University, [Kim Jong-il] was especially kind to me and I treated him cordially as the son of the leader. He was quite smart and full of curiosity and asked me many questions about the curriculum at the university. He often remained behind without following his father to official functions. On those occasions, we talked a lot. My impression of him was that he had a big ambition for power even at that age.
>
> He paid special attention in taking care of his father. He assisted him every morning to the door when he went out. He even helped him put on his shoes. Kim Il-sung was 47 and healthy and had no need to be assisted in that way, but he was nevertheless satisfied with his son's attention.
>
> When Kim Il-sung returned, Kim Jong-il assembled aides, doctors and nurses and instructed them to brief him. There were politburo members among Kim Il-sung's entourage, but they obliged. It was beyond common sense that the junior Kim was conducting his father's business and giving such instructions.
>
> It crossed my mind that maybe someday this boy would seize power by driving out his uncle Kim Yong-ju. One day, he asked me to take him to the exhibition of Russian agriculture and technology. I had a difficult time translating as he asked me so many technical questions. I asked him why he was so interested in technical things

and he answered, "Because my father is very interested in those matters."[10]

Kim Jong-il's serious strategizing about his future began (I want to believe, because I just love the North Korean propaganda) with a fishing trip in 1971. According to one biography, "The Secretary," as he was known then, went with some aides to Mt. Paekdu.[11] It was fall, when the Korean peninsula flares with glorious color. One of the aides noticed The Secretary staring at the water for an age, oblivious to the bobbing of his float, a telltale sign that he'd caught a fish. Hearing steps, he looked up. Just to see how well we're beginning to understand him, let's guess what he might have said:

A. "I am to be a pisher of men, not of pish." (Note that there's no 'f' in Korean). "This pish on my line symbolizes my pather, but bepore I reel it in, I must drown the pish. That's why I'm holding the little pucker underwater."
B. "We have yet to formulate the revolutionary thought of the President as Kimilsungism, although the *Juche* idea has captivated hundreds of millions of people throughout the world."
C. "Another brandy, Jeeves."

Need some help? Let's read on. "After several years of thinking," the book says, "The Secretary finally and resolutely made a historic declaration before our era." I quote:

We live in a new era, the era of *Juche*, which is basically distinguished from the preceding historical periods.

Our era, the era of *Juche*, is, before anything else, a new historical era in which the masses of people have made their debut as masters of their own destiny, as masters of the world for the first time in history.

The era of *Juche* is an entirely new era when the masses of people develop history and shape their own destiny independently and creatively.

Kimilsungism is a new original, great idea on revolution which came into being, reflecting the requirements of the *Juche* era.

In short, he renamed the country's *Juche* ideology "Kimilsungism." In the rebranding speech, he defined the new thought as "a system of the idea, theory and method of *Juche*... a comprehensive system of the *Juche* idea, theory and method of revolution and construction elucidated by this idea... [which] provides the genuine leading principle, theory and leadership method for the revolution of our era, the *Juche* era." The worst thing about this gibberish was that it was foisted with rigor upon the poor North Koreans, who are still required to study it at school, work, army camp, prison, and at home.

In justifying this intellectual battering of the North Korean mind, Kim Jong-il said: "To Kimilsungize the whole society is to train all its members into Kimilsungists infinitely loyal to the President, transform it thoroughly in a way required by Kimilsungism and capture the ideological and material fortresses of Communism."

Although not made public until later, Kim Jong-il was voted in as a secretary of the Party's Central Committee in 1973 and as a member of the Political Committee of the Central Committee in the following year. At the time, the media began referring to him simply as the "Party Center." Party officials fanned out across the country to tell people the good news that Jong-il was to be the successor. He led the "Three Revolutions Movement" and various "speed campaigns." In his effort to demonstrate loyalty and build his political foundation, he gave new shape to the personality cult and, as we have seen, led lavish construction projects to honor his father.

Finally, at a rare Party congress in 1980, Kim Jong-il's position as the successor to Kim Il-sung was made official.

He then became number four in the Politburo, number two in the Party Secretariat, and number three in the Party's Military Commission. He was 38.

In his book *The Guerilla Dynasty*, Adrian Buzo, an Australian scholar who was a diplomat in Pyongyang in the mid-1970s, notes that Kim Jong-il's formal emergence came with the publicizing of his very own "on-the-spot guidance" tours.[12] Kim Il-sung had been doing these for years. It was his way of micro-managing the affairs of the nation. From the pictures, giving on-the-spot guidance doesn't look too difficult. Basically, you make sure you've got officials with notebooks paying attention and then every time the camera is on you, you point at something, and that's where the factory or whatever it is gets built. Buzo notes that Kim Jong-il's tours to places such as the Pyongyang Circus and the People's Palace of Culture received the same banner headlines that his father got. However, Buzo writes, "While the media often described his father's inspection tours in vigorous, even quasi-military language, it described the younger Kim's visits in counterpoint softer language, stressing a benevolent, caring nature."

This fits. For years, the artists and writers and North Korean Hollywood types he hung out with had been singing a song about him (to the tune of U2's "Beautiful Day," if you like):

In the morning when the sky is aglow
We think of your kindly smile.
In the quiet night when the stars shine in the sky
We long for your warm love.

We swear to our dear leader
Pursuing the will of the great President.
However violent the rain, wind or blizzard,
We pledge our loyalty generation after generation.[13]

And so, with this song, Kim Jong-il, the "Party Center," became known as the "Dear Leader," and his picture was nailed up beside that of his father in millions of offices and homes throughout the land.

But, as we have noted, even after his formal anointing, had the Dear Successor made the wrong move, his picture could easily have been removed and another put in its place. Particularly that of Pyong-il, his half-brother. Kim Jong-il's stepmother would not have needed much ammunition to convince Kim Il-sung and his closest associates that Jong-il was the wrong choice.

For this reason, the story of Kim Jong-il's first love, the movie star Sung Hae-rim, became the best-kept secret in the country. While the couple sometimes had sleepovers in Kim Il-sung's villas when father was not around, Kim Il-sung never knew of the extent of this relationship. Our relatively detailed knowledge of it comes from Hae-rim's sister, Sung Hae-rang, and her two children, all of whom escaped from North Korea.[14]

The affair began when Jong-il was 26 and Hae-rim was 31.[15] Sung Hae-rim was a well-known actress, which may explain the frequency of Jong-il's visits to the movie set, and indeed his interest in movie-making. She had been unhappily married to the son of a South Korean novelist who had sided with the North Koreans during the Korean War, and had a daughter who was already in her early teens. After completing a movie called *Fate of a Volunteer*, she divorced her husband, quit acting and secretly began dating Kim Jong-il. She entered the relationship in part to help her father's position. Her mother was an editor at the Party newspaper, *Rodong Shinmun*, but her South Korean-born father was treated with suspicion because he had been a landowner. However, she had genuine feelings for Kim Jong-il, according to her sister. The fact that he grew up without his own mother stirred her affection.

No one knows for sure whether they went through a marriage ceremony or not, but they lived together through the 1970s and 1980s. To keep the relationship from all but a few trusted associates, Kim Jong-il threw up a wall of secrecy. In 1976, he asked Hae-rim's sister, Hae-rang, who was a widow, to move in with her two children and her mother and to tutor the couple's secret lovechild. At that time the boy, Kim Jong-nam, was five years old and had to be schooled at home, lest the identity of his father slip out.[16] They lived lavishly in remote villas, with absurd amounts of money spent on the child. Jong-nam had a massive 990 square meter playroom that was restocked each year with toys bought from overseas by "gift-purchase teams" from division two, department nine, of Kim Jong-il's personal security staff.

"To touch all the toys would take a day," Jong-nam's cousin, Lee Han-yong, wrote.

In a scene straight out of a movie, Jong-nam, then four, was once being treated in a hospital when the Dear Leader's stepmother, Kim Song-ae, and half-brother, Kim Pyong-il, arrived on an official tour of the facility. His grandmother quickly hoisted Jong-nam onto her back, sneaked out the window and hid behind some trees until the official tour was over.

As he was growing up, Kim Jong-il felt that Jong-nam was suffering from the isolation and allowed mother, aunt and the boy to spend time in houses in Geneva and Moscow. He grew up to be artistic like his father and, despite the cloak and dagger life, optimistic and humorous by nature.[17] He's had his share of trouble, though. When he was a teenager, Jong-nam suffered his father's wrath, ironically over an unsanctioned girlfriend. In fact, Kim Jong-il was so angry about this that he threatened to send Jong-nam to work in the coalmines. In 2001, Jong-nam caused some embarrassment when he was very publicly expelled from Japan for trying to enter the country on a forged Dominican Republic passport issued in the Chinese name Pan Xiong. He reportedly said that he had wanted to take his son to Tokyo Disneyland.

Jong-nam's mother, Sung Hae-rim, died in 2002 in Moscow.

The relationship with Sung Hae-rim appears to represent Kim Jong-il's "fatal flaw," the weakness that should have been his undoing. But he managed to keep it from damaging his political life, even when, in the early 1970s, Kim Il-sung told his son it was time he should marry and, unaware of Sung Hae-rim, selected the daughter of a military officer for him. Jong-il obediently married her. And so he maintained a parallel household with his official wife, Kim Young-sook, who bore him a daughter, Kim Sol-song, and possibly another child.

Outside of these two relationships, Kim Jong-il is said to have had a few liaisons. Among the rumors from defectors is one that has him sleeping with an actress who resembled his mother. Another claims he had a sexual relationship with a classmate, even after she married, for the same reason.[18] He reportedly had a daughter, Kim Hye-kyong, with another mistress named Hong Il-chon.

We also know that in the early 1980s he took up with Ko Young-hee, a Japanese-born Korean whom he met when she was in a state dance troupe. Again, it is not known if he formally divorced Young-sook to marry her, but Young-hee bore him two boys, Jong-chul and Jong-oon, and is today assumed to be his wife. Recent propaganda referring to her as "respected mother" suggests that one of them is being groomed for the top job. Analysts assume it to be Jong-chul, now in his 20s, but there is one report that reckons the second boy is his father's favorite.[19]

One of the ironies of Kim Jong-il's public emergence as official successor in the early 1980s is that, by this time, he was already in fact increasingly becoming the real power in North Korea. His father was taking more and more of a symbolic role. It is possible that all state documents requiring Kim Il-sung's attention went through Kim Jong-il first from as early as 1976.[20]

Kim Jong-il was not present when former US president Jimmy Carter met with Kim Il-sung in June 1994, but he is understood to have been closely involved in the meeting. For example, during a meeting on a boat, Kim Il-sung said he would get back to Carter on the former president's request for the return of the remains of US soldiers killed during the Korean War. Hearing of this, Kim Jong-il asked his stepmother, who was on the boat, to go into the cabin and suggest to Kim Il-sung that he accept the request.[21]

Kim Il-sung died of a heart attack in July 1994. He was at a villa in the Myohyang Mountain area, near the Yongbyun nuclear site, at the time of his death. There are unconfirmed reports that the heart attack was brought on by an argument with Kim Jong-il. There are also reports that a helicopter with a medical team crashed and that at least one pilot was shot. Whatever the truth of this, the death seemed to shock Kim Jong-il and his sister, Kyung-hee. She could be observed among mourners on TV quite beside herself with grief. "Kim Jong-il used to confine himself to his room for a long time during those days," according to a former chef. His wife, Ko Young-hee, found him with a pistol, he said.[22]

It says something of his secretive political style that when his father died, there was serious doubt overseas as to whether Kim Jong-il would be able to maintain power. Kim Il-sung had gone to the grave having just promised Jimmy Carter he would resume stalled talks with the United States on the nuclear weapons question and with South Korea toward arranging a summit. But Kim Young-sam, the South's president, decided to drop the idea of a summit to avoid strengthening Jong-il's hold on power. Actually, as it later turned out, there was no doubt as to who was in charge, but the succession was not formalized for another three years, giving the perception overseas of a nation adrift.

But far from flakiness, this secrecy served to turn weakness into strength. It was during this period that mounting food shortages devastated the country. By appearing to engage in a three-year mourning period, Jong-il could avoid direct blame while demonstrating his loyalty to his father in a way that resonated with Korean tradition. "How can I succeed the leader when he is still alive?" he said on the fiftieth anniversary of the Korean Workers' Party in 1995.[23] Already chairman of the all-powerful National Defense Commission, he took the post of general secretary of the Party in December 1997. He did not take the less important post of the presidency, but instead declared his dead father, "President for Eternity."

Dear Boy: *Kim Jong-il went by the Russian nickname of "Shura" for the first few years of his life.*

Pre-bouffant Days: *An undated photograph of a younger and leaner Kim Jong-il, sporting a more mainstream hairstyle than his current luxuriant cut.*

Jolly Leader: *The young Kim Jong-il enjoys a laugh and a cigarette. He's since given up smoking.*

Dear Successor: *From the mid-1970s Kim Jong-il took increasing power behind the scenes. Here he watches as his father inspects some documents.*

Father and Son: *An early propaganda photo of Kim Il-sung (right) and Kim Jong-il (left). Note the portly pose conveying confidence and authority.*

Communist Dynasty: *On official occasions, pictures of Kim Il-sung, left, and Kim Jong-il take precedence over the flag and other symbols of state.*

Family Affair: *Sung Hae-rang (top left) and her children (standing) moved in as well when Kim Jong-il took up with her sister, Hae-rim. Kim poses in this early 80s picture with his and Hae-rim's love child, Kim Jong-nam (seated).*

The Odd Couple: *Kim Jong-il poses with Park Geun-hye, the daughter of the late South Korean strongman, Park Chung-hee. Herself a leading politican in Seoul, Ms Park visited North Korea in 2002 before revelations of Kim's continuing nuclear program made such visits unfashionable.*

US Visitor: In 2000, then US Secretary of State Madeleine Albright became the highest-ranking serving official to ever visit North Korea.

Two Kims: *Kim Jong-il and South Korean President Kim Dae-jung during their historic June 2000 summit in Pyongyang. Kim Dae-jung's bold initiative won him the Nobel Peace Prize. Within two years, the thrill of this moment would be lost amid revelations of the North's nuclear weapons program and evidence that the South paid hundreds of millions of dollars for the summit.*

Border Patrol: *South Korean soldiers check the border fence at the De-Militarized Zone — actually a very heavily militarized zone that vies with Indo-Pakistan as the globe's tensest border — separating the two Koreas.*

Military Support: *Kim Jong-il, reacting here to an unseen crowd, takes pains to demonstrate the close support he appears to enjoy from the top brass.*

Night Vision: *Even in Pyongyang there is not enough energy to light up the buildings and streets at night.*

Pyongyang View: *A panoramic shot taken from the Juche Tower across the Daedong River, showing the showcase capital in all its splendor. The square in the center is called — not surprisingly — Kim Il Sung Square.*

Free Zone: *North Korea's latest economic zone plan calls for fencing off the town of Sinniju on the Chinese border. It is unlikely that any such plans will really take off under the current communist government.*

Nuclear Games: *North Korea's nuclear facilities, like this one at Yongbynn, has put the country on a collision course with the United States.*

Spy Camera: *Aerial shot of nuclear facilities at Yongbyun.*

Dear Kidnapper: Kim Jong-il poses with South Korean director Shin Sang-ok and actress Choi Eun-hee, whose kidnapping he arranged in a bizaare bid to upgrade the North Korean movie industry.

The Price of Failure: Severely malnourished toddlers — three among millions — is vivid testimony to the human tragedy that has engulfed the people of North Korea under the leadership of Kim Jong-il.

Grimace Please: *Unlike the exuberant South Koreans, who lark about and flash v-signs when the cameras are out, North Koreans seem grim and unhappy by comparison. Here a family group poses in front of the main statue of Kim Il-sung in Pyongyang.*

6

Portrait of the Artist

Kim Jong-il is an arty fellow. Before he emerged as the successor, he seems to have spent a lot of time making movies and producing plays.

During one of my trips to North Korea, I saw a sign at the film studios in Pyongyang recording how many times the Dear Leader had visited to give on-the-spot guidance. I was told there were seven such studios around the country, and based on the dodgy assumption that this was true and that he visited each one with equal frequency (it is more likely that the one I went to was Chick Central and that this was where he spent all his time), I figured that in his heyday in the 1960s and 1970s, he was on one set or another every two days over a span of two decades. That's passion.

His film background, far from making him the Ronald Reagan of North Korea, has been used by a foreign analyst to prove he's a flake who can't distinguish between art and reality. But this conclusion misses the propaganda importance of the arts. Just as he sharpened *Juche* into Kimilsungism, so Kim Jong-il's contribution to the arts rallied the creative soul of the nation to his own filial cause: worship of his father.

Among the 1970s movies and musicals for which Kim Jong-il is alleged to have written librettos or otherwise worked on are the revolutionary opera, *The Sea of Blood* (*Pibada*) — no, I'm not making this up, it's been performed overseas — *True Daughter of the Party, Flower Girl,* and *Fate of a Member of the Self-Defense Corps.*

Two books, which are available in the West, help to illuminate his thinking in this field: *Kim Jong-il On the Art of the Cinema* and *Kim Jong-il On the Art of Opera,* apparently based on speeches given in April 1973 and September 4–6, 1974, respectively. I would like to quote at length from these immortal works, not because they're any good, but because it's important to walk a mile in a North Korean citizen's moccasins to get a feel for their required reading.

From *On the Art of Opera*:

Establishing *Juche* in opera art means solving all the problems relating to the creation of operas to meet the interests of the revolution in one's own country and of one's own people and to suit the specific situation in one's own country and the sentiments of one's nation.[1]

To explore what this means in practice, we should consider *The Sea of Blood.* It's a revolutionary opera all right. The title refers to Manchuria during the Japanese occupation. It "describes the historical background of the 1930s truthfully because the portrayal of the life of the heroine's family is not confined to the bounds of family affairs but covers a broad field of politics, the economy, the military and culture, while exposing the true nature of society at that time."[2] The songs in *The Sea of Blood* do not contain words of Chinese origin and other "puzzling words," something Kim Jong-il advises against. (In Korean, there is frequently a choice of a pure Korean word and a Koreanized version of the Chinese character. South Koreans mix them up but northerners don't learn Chinese characters. Aside from ideological concepts, this is the main way language use differs in the two halves of the peninsula).

Enough of opera. I prefer *On the Art of Cinema,* not just

because I've never been to the opera, but because each chapter begins with a quote from Kim Il-sung. This one kicks off the chapter, "Guiding the Creative Process":

> When the Party's line and policies are correct and proper means and measures are adopted for their implementation, success in the implementation of the revolutionary tasks depends entirely on what work methods and styles the officials directly responsible for their implementation employ and on how they mobilize the broad masses in this work.[3]

I had to read this sentence four times to get a grip on it. I think it means, "If you get a good idea for a movie, it will bomb if the director sucks and people don't buy the video."

Another Kim Il-sung quote, this time for the "Art and Creative Endeavor" chapter:

> You, the film makers, must thoroughly revolutionize yourselves and fight on devotedly for the Party and the revolution, for the victory of the cause of socialism and communism. This is the way to prove yourself worthy of the Party's consideration and the trust it places in you.[4]

In these books, Kim Jong-il gets down to the basics of artistic endeavor. For example, consider this on movie music:

> Film music should provide a clear emotional characterization of the ideological content of the production and the ideas and emotions of the characters. Music which does this will be quite distinctive, and its emotional tone will be unequivocal.[5]

He goes on to point out that if songs in movies about the working class have "militant" melodies, they will lack originality and will "fail to add a fresh and distinctive emotional tone to the film." It's better to mix up "melodies which are militant, lyrical, noble, or merry" to suit the characters and the development of the plot.

There's more.

"In life a song is never far from us," he writes. "A song has such a great ideological and emotional influence on people that it stirs people's hearts and inspires them in the struggle to create a new life."[6] Kim Jong-il says that to produce good songs, you first need good lyrics which are both "poetic and, at the same time, rich in ideological content." He advises songwriters to balance songs about present happiness with memories of past struggle. If there's too much joy and happiness, there's a risk the lyrics may be "tainted with hedonism."

"While they sing of this life, the lyrics should ensure that people do not forget their former miserable plight, and so inspire them with the burning desire and the enthusiastic commitment to hasten towards a brighter future," he says, adding that, "When singing of the joy of nature, too, lyrics should reflect the advantages of the socialist system and the noble life of our people, emphasizing their revolutionary spirit."

You can tell that he's thought these issues through. The objective, of course, is not art, but the harnessing of sentimentality to the cause of the revolution. The Korean communist revolution is an expression of anger at colonial suppression, but the insecurity it aimed to overcome is expressed at almost every turn. Consider this on orchestra formation:

> When we speak of combining Korean and Western musical instruments we have in mind laying the main accent on the former, subordinating the latter to the Korean music, emphasizing the specific features of our woodwind instruments so as to make the unique tonality of our national instruments clearly audible and properly combining the different kinds of musical instruments. If the principle of *Juche* is not observed in forming an orchestra, and various kinds of instruments are mixed

together on an egalitarian footing, the sound will become confused and make it impossible to preserve the unique national tonality of our music.[7]

As you read through this, you start to get a sense of the issues that may have been facing the North Korean movie industry at the time. This comment may have addressed a hot debate between people who felt that nationalism was best expressed with uniquely Korean instruments, while others thought that North Korea should demonstrate its advancement by having musicians dress up in tuxedos and play the violin.

I suspect there was a similar debate in the make-up department. Get this:

"Make-up is a noble art since it unifies the external appearances of the actor and the character and creates a new human image," writes Kim. "If make-up artists attempt to create a character portrayal by thinking only of the character's personality, and give no thought to the actor's essential features, they cannot help the actor, and the make-up is reduced to a mere superficial display."[8]

If, like me, you feel that our society focuses too much on the private lives of celebrities, you'll find some bits of Kim's thoughts refreshing, such as, "The actor is an artist who contributes, through his portrayal of a character, to deepening people's understanding of life and the situation and to re-educating them in a revolutionary manner."[9]

Other bits are iffier.

"What matters in art and literature is how life is observed and described," he writes. "If art is to show a meaningful life, it must seek that life in the struggle of communist people of a new type and depict it in all its depth." He gets rather carried away with this one:

No one is so sincere and loves life so ardently as a communist. Communists are revolutionaries who always know how to create a new life wherever they are. Their emotions are more profound and humane than those of other people. This is why, wherever the communist people of the new type are growing up, life is always vigorous, vibrant, overflowing with revolutionary optimism, diverse and rich.[10]

Even if this is true, though, it's not easy for an artist to capture that superior communist vigor. Some authors, he says, write "exclusively — and boringly — about military combat actions in an attempt to portray the struggle of revolutionaries. This is a mistake. Revolutionaries are not the kind of people who regard their struggle and their lives as two separate things. Life and struggle always mean one and the same thing to revolutionaries who are devoted to the revolution and construction and whose belief in communism is firm."

To make his point he cites the Prefect One: "As the great leader Comrade Kim Il Sung has said, the life of a revolutionary begins with struggle and ends with struggle. For revolutionaries, life consists of their struggle and the struggle is their life." I guess for the modern revolutionary, the main struggle is struggling through this kind of stuff every day.

In a section in *On the Art of Cinema* entitled, "The Characteristics of the Wide Screen Should be Used Effectively," there is some depth to Kim Jong-il's thinking. You wonder if this was not produced by a ghost-writer:

The expanded screen space of the wide-screen film offers abundant potential for a broader reflection of life and for depicting objects with greater definition of form and perspective, so that life is depicted the way people see it in reality... Some people attempt to exploit the advantages of the wide screen by presenting nothing but large images of objects and crowding a lot of things into a single frame. In doing this they are thinking of nothing but the scale and form of the screen and ignoring the requirements of the content to be presented on it... Whatever forms are used in art, the content must not be trimmed to fit within a frame. Life provides the content of art, and the content demands a suitable form... When the form of a piece of work is regarded as good, it is because it matches the content, which has been expressed in an excellent and distinctive fashion, and not because the form itself has some appeal of its own apart from the content... A literary work is not regarded as a masterpiece because of its scale, but because of its content; in camerawork, also, it is not the physical scale but the expression of content that should be broad.[11]

After a few years of trying to guide the movie industry, Kim Jong-il must have become frustrated with the lack of progress, for some time around 1977 he ordered the kidnapping of a top South Korean movie director and his actress wife. These southern stars would be used to educate their northern brothers and sisters in how to make really good movies.

Shin Sang-ok had fallen foul of dictator Park Chung-hee in the South.[12] Marked a dissident for complaining about censorship and bribery, the South Korean government closed down his movie company. This news may have given Kim Jong-il the idea that he might be amenable to defecting. Jong-il's original strategy appears to have been to kidnap Choi Eun-hee, a leading actress and Shin's ex-wife, to lure Shin. They had recently divorced after 23 years of marriage, but remained close both personally and professionally. In an elaborate plot, Choi was invited in early 1978 by movie business associates to Hong Kong where she was kidnapped and taken on an eight-day boat journey from Repulse Bay to the North Korean port of Nampo.

In a scene that will no doubt one day itself be included in a movie, for it highlights so vividly the extent to which North Korea is in moral outer space, Kim Jong-il himself turned up at the dock to meet the kidnapped celebrity off the boat.

"Thank you for coming, Madame Choi. I am Kim Jong-il," he said, as if she'd responded to an ad. He then invited her to sit in the back of his black limo and tried to make small talk. When they reached Pyongyang, he started pointing out the sights. "Kim was as happy as a general making a triumphant entrance into the capital," she recalled.

Choi was taken to a luxurious house, which she later found out was one of Kim's personal villas. There, before Kim left, one of his aides asked her to hand over her South Korean passport and ID card. That night she called out the names of her children and cried herself to sleep.

Kim Jong-il was an attentive kidnapper. That first morning, he sent flowers. He also sent a doctor who would come every day to check on her. One of the phones in the villa was a direct line to Kim Jong-il. He started inviting her to small dinner parties. He got some stylish traditional Korean *hanbok* outfits for her, and later said he had showed the pictures of her wearing them to Kim Il-sung. The Great Leader allegedly remarked that she looked beautiful and, after that, she was required to wear the traditional clothes for every party. She worried that she would be presented to Kim Il-sung as a plaything.

At one party, Kim Jong-il introduced Choi to a woman called Chong Kyong-hui. The woman, she was told, was the deputy of the organization responsible for espionage and terrorism against South Korea. The terrorist chief looked at the glamorous Choi with cold, jealous eyes. "Let's work for revolution," she said and Kim Jong-il chuckled as if enjoying the irony.

Choi was invited every Friday to a party in Pyongyang to watch movies. Guests would dance the fox trot or disco to a live band, or play blackjack or *mahjong*, and listen to and sing South Korean songs until morning. Kim Jong-il didn't dance and sing himself, but just watched. He'd often interrupt the band to get them to play another tune and sometimes he'd get up and conduct. Regular partygoers included his sister, Kyong-hee, her husband Chang Song-taek, intelligence officials, Workers' Party official Kim Yong-soon and the foreign minister, Ho Dam. On one occasion, Kim Jong-il asked Choi to sing a song by the South Korean singer Patti Kim. Halfway through, she began to think of her ex-husband Shin Sang-ok and tears rolled down her face. The partygoers went quiet. One, thinking she'd forgotten the words, prompted her, demonstrating knowledge of enemy culture that would have landed an ordinary North Korean in jail. She finished to applause.

At these parties, Choi says, guests would be required to knock back a glass of cognac upon arrival. (Although Kim Jong-il has since eased up on his own drinking, apparently this is still his style of loosening up guests). The idea of Kim Jong-il forcing his guests to drink suggests a rather bullying hale-fellow-well-met character. At men-only drinking parties amounts consumed are said to have been enormous. Choi learned from another guest how to spit the liquor out when no one was looking. As an indication of how proud Kim Jong-il was of having Choi in the North and of the effort to win her over, he even invited her to his home to join his family celebrating his birthday.

At one point, she asked him if he could send her home to Seoul. He was quiet for a moment and asked her to be patient.

"The problem will soon be resolved," he said rather enigmatically.

Although a kidnap victim, Choi was also in Kim's mind a guest and accomplished actress. In this latter capacity, she was free to give Kim Jong-il her views on North Korean art. After seeing *The Sea of Blood*, for example, she told him she thought the music and costumes were inappropriate. She also ventured the idea that other themes besides revolution could inspire people. Like love. The story would be better with a love interest, she suggested.

"When director Shin gets here, we can figure it out," he replied. Shin had recently visited and planned to return, Kim said. Choi was stunned to hear this. She would later learn that his "visit" and "plan to return" were not exactly true. He was, in fact, in a North Korean prison.

At the time of Choi's disappearance in Hong Kong, Shin had been experiencing financial and professional difficulties and decided to apply to emigrate to the US. En route to the US, Shin went to Hong Kong. Although he asked a business contact in Hong Kong to report Choi's disappearance, it is typical of South Koreans' lack of faith in their police, even today, that he then set about making his own inquiries. He continued on to the States and there enlisted the advice of Kim Hong-wook, a former South Korean CIA chief who was living in exile after having turned against Park Chung-hee. After arriving in the States, Shin filed his application for permanent US residency and left the US for Hong Kong. By now, the Korean police and media were convinced that Shin, with his financial difficulties, was behind the disappearance. After Korean consulate officials in Hong Kong tried to get him to hand over his passport, he decided to seek the protection of the Hong Kong police.

Unaware of his business associate's connection with North Korean agents, Shin was lured in the same way as Choi and kidnapped.

Shin and Choi were kept at separate locations, each unaware that the other was alive and now in North Korea. While Choi was frequently in tears of despair, Shin dreamed of freedom. Five months after his kidnapping, Shin escaped in a car from the guesthouse in which he was being kept. After a long drive, he ditched the vehicle and made his way to a railroad station, where he hid among crates of explosives until he was able to sneak aboard a freight train. The next morning he was caught. A strange, almost comical questioning followed, with interrogators writing down one answer at a time, leaving the room and returning to ask another question. Shin concluded they were on the line to Kim Jong-il and that the Dear Leader was effectively conducting a long-distance interrogation. Had Shin lied and said he went for a joyride, he might have been returned to his guesthouse. However, he told them he was trying to get to Hong Kong because he couldn't stand living in North Korea any more. He was taken to jail where he was kept in solitary confinement for over three months. After another failed escape attempt, he was formally indicted and sent to a camp for political prisoners. In February 1983, after serving almost four years, Shin was released.

Unaware of these events, Choi had been living in relative comfort, although she had not had any contact with Kim Jong-il for around three years. Unexpectedly, Kim then started inviting her to his parties again. Choi was at a dinner party in March 1983 when Shin arrived surrounded by several officials. They stared at each other in amazement until Kim Jong-il said, "Well, go ahead and hug each other. Why are you just standing there?" They hugged and the guests applauded.

"All right, stop hugging and come over here," Kim instructed. When the Dear Leader announced that Shin was to be his movie adviser, the guests applauded some more.

"Let's have a wedding ceremony for you on April fifteenth, the Great Leader's birthday," he said, suggesting that they remarry. The Dear Leader was so happy that he ignored doctor's orders and had a few drinks.

"Mr Shin, please forgive the dramatics," Kim Jong-il said, placing Shin's hand on his knee and squeezing it. "I'm sorry to have caused you so much suffering. No one ever laid a hand on Madame Choi. Now, I send her back to you exactly as she was. Mr Shin, we communists are pure. Aren't we, comrades?" The noisy crowd responded in the affirmative and the cognac started to flow. The party lasted till 3 a.m.

The surreal quality of this whole situation cannot be understated. Choi says she still finds it difficult to understand

Kim Jong-il's thinking, but for Shin, who had seen the rough side of prison but who had also experienced the humanity of North Koreans even in that environment, there was a simpler explanation for their kidnapping that lay in the values system of North Korea's communist elite. "The revolution justifies everything," he said. "They think that anyone who lives in a capitalist country can be satisfied if they have enough money. Kim Jong-il was building a new luxury mansion for us and a new movie set like Hollywood was almost completed by the time we escaped. He believed that with all the material support he was providing us, we would be happy."[13]

An additional blind spot for the North Korean leader, Shin thinks, is that he doesn't understand freedom. As difficult as this may be to appreciate, he is not alone. Political freedom and the rights of the individual are relatively new arrivals in many parts of the world. Freedom is a new concept even in South Korea, where people now in their forties remember when they could have their long hair forcibly cut on the street by police, when they could be arrested for criticizing the government, when articles on Korea in the foreign press were blacked out of newspapers, and when those with power took their right to abuse it for granted. Indeed, in abusing power, they called on higher and more familiar virtues of "national interest" and "stability," and felt that freedom was synonymous with chaos.

In North Korea, Choi met a Chinese woman who had been kidnapped from Macao, and heard of a similar case of a French woman lured by a male agent. Kim Hyun-hee, the commando who blew up a South Korean airliner in 1987, told her captors in Seoul that North Koreans had abducted her Japanese language trainer at the Keumsung Military College from a beach in Japan while she was playing with her children.[14]

Kim Jong-il may have felt kidnapping was a good thing to do, and expected that Choi and Shin would also see the light. He obviously thought they had, for he gave them an annual US$2 million budget, passports and the freedom to travel, and permitted them to write to their families. He even explained at length why he had kidnapped them — to develop the North Korean movie industry — a conversation that the South Korean couple secretly tape-recorded.

In their eight years in North Korea, they say, they thought of escape every day. Finally, on a trip to Europe in 1986, they evaded their bodyguards and sought asylum at the US embassy. Once in a safe house in Vienna, an American official handed Choi Eun-hee a pink rose and said, "Welcome to the West."

She burst into tears.

Is Kim Jong-il Evil?

When told he'd become something of a star in South Korea after the inter-Korean summit of 2000, Kim Jong-il's own analysis was, "After I appeared on TV screens, I'm sure, they came to know that I am not like a man with horns on the head."[1]

Which raises the question. Does he? Have horns on his head? In other words, is Kim Jong-il evil?

This is an important question because our answer will help us predict his actions and guide us in how to deal with him. But how should we define evil? If we take the popular, subjective use of the word, as it may appear in tabloid headlines, Kim Jong-il surely is an evil leader. He enslaves his people and threatens his neighbors with nuclear weaponry. What more evidence do we need? But we should be careful of this use of the word, because, more than any other, it justifies demonizing and sets us on a dulling of the conscience that could end with civilized folk like you and me, dear reader, whooping and high-fiving as our boys bomb his cities. As offensive as his regime may seem in the modern world, we should not assume that the leader of an undemocratic state is necessarily evil, any more than European kings were evil in the pre-democracy period.

We need to look closer at Kim Jong-il the individual. The problem, as we have seen, is that there is insufficient evidence in the form of personal writings and memoirs of associates to allow us to figure what may lie in his heart, to guess the state of his conscience and how it might operate upon his feelings and behavior, to know the beliefs that inform him. If he was truly evil, his own therapist, if he has one, might not reach that diagnosis for a while because evil wraps itself in lies and confusion. Those closest to him, who would be our best sources, might well think he's a great chap. Could he be evil in the sense that he is a murderous man, a liar, a deadened heart who seeks to control and suppress others? Did he seal his power over the decades to exercise a monstrous nature? Or was he born to the position, as a prince is born to kingship? In which case, is he a decent prince struggling in a brutish kingdom; an enlightened prince of, er, darkness? Or even a liberal democrat struggling in a communist body? Or is he an angry, violent prince, such as Saddam Hussein's first son, Uday, who was locked up for beating one of his father's aides to death? Could he even be demonic, "possessed of the beast"?

Or, if he is not exactly evil, could he be mad?

Jerrold M. Post, who has conducted political psychology profiles for the CIA, thinks the Dear Leader is a nutter. The indications are, Post believes, that Kim has the "core characteristics of the most dangerous personality disorder, malignant narcissism."[2] His pampered upbringing has created a warped figure with an extreme degree of self-absorption, a grandiose view of himself, and a commensurate inability to empathize with others and to understand the United States, South Korea, and Japan, Post argues. This is all evidenced by his insensitivity to the people's suffering, his lavish lifestyle, humiliation as a means of control over his inner circle, a paranoid sense that he is surrounded by enemies, and a willingness to use aggression to eliminate them. Post's conclusion is that this lethal mixture could lead to political miscalculation. In other words, this wacko could press the nuclear button.

But I wonder if there is not some cultural misinterpretation here. Take, for example, the idea of "humiliation." When Kim Jong-il's people enter his presence they bow deeply and don't straighten up until he signals that they can. In his presence they also refer to him in the third person as the "Dear Leader" or "Our Supreme Commander."[3] Are they being humiliated? If they were Americans, we would have to say yes. But, like it or not, this is how it is in the authoritarian Korean political culture on both sides of the DMZ. Subordinates bow and scrape around presidents, conglomerate heads and gang bosses (at least in TV dramas) in South Korea. A government minister in Seoul was once bowing as he walked backwards, departing the presence of President Kim Young-sam (ruled 1993–98), when he tripped over.

On one occasion, Kim Jong-il invited Hwang Jang-yop, the one-time dean of Kim Il-sung University and a Workers' Party secretary, to a party. "I really want to see Secretary Hwang having a drink!" Jong-il announced.

> At this, everybody tried to pour drinks in my mouth. I closed my mouth tight and the drink flowed onto my clothes. After they'd given up, [Kim Jong-il's sister] Kim Kyong-hee tried to make me drink. In order not to embarrass her, I swallowed some. Then Kim Jong-il said, "Stop! I will make him drink!" He took a bottle in front of him and filled my glass and said, "You should have treated everybody equally. It's not fair to only give favor to her." I thought he was right and closed my eyes and gulped it down my throat. To my great astonishment, it was plain water slightly colored to make it look like liquor. Maybe he was following the recommendation of his doctors not to drink. But, nobody knew this.[4]

From a western perspective, if we imagine ourselves in Hwang's position, perhaps we would feel "humiliated." But from a Korean perspective, Kim Jong-il was behaving like a real boss — getting public obedience, but actually taking Hwang's aversion to drinking into consideration.

And what about his security paranoia? Is this a symptom of malignant narcissism or reasonable threat? There have been rumors of attempts on his life, including one in 2002, but we do not know for sure how true they are. Does he believe that the CIA, the South Koreans, or one day the Chinese, might try to assassinate him? I would think so, especially as he has sent agents against South Korean targets: the attempted assassination of Chun Doo-hwan (ruled 1980–88) in Burma in 1983, in which several of Chun's government ministers and officials were killed; and the 1987 bombing of the Korean airliner in an attempt to encourage the Soviet bloc to boycott the 1988 Seoul Olympics.

According to a former bodyguard, Lee Yeong-kook, who defected to South Korea, Kim Jong-il's movements are kept secret and it is only announced that he has visited a location after he has left.[5] Kim Jong-il often lectures his bodyguards himself, Lee Yeong-kook says. On those occasions, he might slap them on the shoulder and crack jokes. He once instructed that, while soldiers should be well behaved, his guards should be impeccably mannered because their behavior reflected directly back on him. "You must love my guards like your own sons," he told instructors. "If you do not love them, they will not be inspired to guard me well." Bodyguards were required to have pleasant expressions on their faces and to address each other politely, regardless of rank. This instruction is very revealing of Korean culture. It was issued to avoid fights breaking out between the bodyguards. In their hierarchical culture, Koreans tend to bully juniors, especially in the military. They also tend to be very explosive by nature and retaliate against any perceived slight. Thus, to avoid incidents that might create gaps in his security, he orders them to be nice to one another. Anyone who showed up for work looking sick or angry was taken off duty for fear he would make mistakes. Perceived security threats are dealt with viciously. Once in 1985, guards saw a fishing boat illegally fishing near an east coast villa in which Kim Jong-il was staying. When the guards approached, the crew turned on the engine and tried to escape. Guards shot at them and two men were killed. The guards were worried that they would be accused of overreaction, but when he received the report, Kim Jong-il complimented them for their quick response and presented them with medals.

In his portrayal of Kim Jong-il as a malignant narcissist, Post also cites the Dear Leader's apparent insensitivity to the suffering of others. Frankly, we do not know whether he shed tears over those who died during the famine of the 1990s. It is tempting to speculate that the harsh guerrilla childhood, the longing for his mother and her death left him with an emotionally undeveloped heart that cannot empathize. But if his heart has hardened to his people's suffering, it is more likely to have done so by other strands of thinking. One is the North Korean belief that its economic difficulties are primarily the result of the decades-long US embargo. Therefore, he might think the deaths were a consequence of struggle against the imperialists, i.e. warfare. It's possible, too, that Kim Jong-il considers many of his suffering people to be "non-persons" outside of his sphere of interest. Although Kim Jong-il is the leader of North Korea, his direct sphere of concern, one might say, is the few thousand families that make up the elite. Those who fall outside it perhaps do not evoke his sympathy. Indeed, a significant proportion of the North Korean population is officially classified for reasons of class or background as "hostile" to the communist revolution and to be feared. So, we may assume, reports of famine deaths or of numbers in the gulag do not profoundly affect him. Such is the power of culture and ideology to anaesthetize the conscience.

None of this makes Kim Jong-il, on his own demerits, evil or mad.

What kind of leader is he then?

In approaching this question, I should own up to a bias. As hard as I've tried to shake it, I am suspicious of anyone who would seek political office whereby they can exercise power over others. To reach for the skies in life is healthy. But those who would reach for political power should be brought in for questioning. This bias comes very easily to reporters and underscores the natural tension that exists between journalism and politics. It derives, I think, from the fact that evil involves the misuse of power. And although power exists in any relationship — journalists, too, have a lot of it to abuse — its worst consequences are never so apparent as when it is in the hands of those who run countries and command armies.

That said, what we need to consider is not so much Kim Jong-il the therapy patient, but Kim Jong-il the political leader. In other words, we need to assess his political character. To some extent, with politicians, it is irrelevant whether they are engaged or distant, gentle or harsh, restrained or — and this is an argument I had with many women and Republican men during the Clinton years — randy. What counts for we, the people, is what they do in office.

In his book *The Presidential Character: Predicting Performance in the White House*, James David Barber assesses leaders by two broad measures. The first is their degree of pro-activity. In other words, to what extent do they forge their environment as opposed to being passively pushed along by it? Do they drive policy or have it handed to them by aides? Second, are they driven by a positive or negative disposition?[6] Do they feel life to be a burden, a series of obligations, or do they see it as a sequence of adventures, opportunities, and growth?

Thus, Barber argues, in broad brush, we find four types of American president: active–positive, active–negative, passive–

positive, and passive–negative. The active–positives have goals and are productive in pursuing them. High self-esteem allows them to both enjoy the role and remain flexible when things don't work so well. The downside of this type may be their tendency to emphasize the rational and failure to understand the irrational in politics. Active–positives include John F. Kennedy and Franklin D. Roosevelt. Active–negatives tend to be compulsive and ambitious, and escape into hard work that does not bring the satisfaction they think it will. Barber sees Lyndon Johnson, Herbert Hoover and Woodrow Wilson as such presidents. For passive–positives, life is a "search for affection as a reward for being agreeable and cooperative rather than personally assertive."[7] Leaders in this group, according to Barber, are good people, but, instead of pushing policy, they tend to allow it to be brought to them. He cites Ronald Reagan as an example. Finally, the passive–negatives. From such a label, you'd wonder why such people would make the effort to get there in the first place. The answer, Barber says, is that they feel they have to. They tend to withdraw and become "guardians of the right and proper way, above the sordid politicking of lesser men." Among twentieth-century American presidents, Barber considers Calvin Coolidge and Dwight Eisenhower to fit into this category.

Clearly, it would be best to elect only active–positive presidents. Such leaders want results, Barber says, while active–negatives want power, passive–positives want love, and passive–negatives stress their civic virtue.

Using Barber's system of categorization — and stretching it to include dictators — the evidence we have would strongly indicate that Kim Jong-il is first of all an active leader. In fact, he comes across as almost overly so. On the two of my visits to North Korea in official delegations, the host, Party Secretary Kim Yong-soon, made it very clear that Kim Jong-il was receiving personal reports of our trip. He personally gave the go-ahead to let a CNN crew enter the country in April 1994.

"Kim Jong-il is very involved in everything," says Shin Sang-ok, the kidnapped South Korean movie director. "He knows who's traveling abroad, for example."[8]

In work, Kim Jong-il is something of a night owl, a habit he got from his father. According to a former bodyguard, Kim Jong-il works in his office through the night and returns to his residence at dawn to go to bed. He apparently sleeps only four hours a night and so is up before noon.[9] When his father was alive, he would always phone while he was having brunch to check whether the Great Leader was up and about.[10] The first time he took the kidnapped actress Choi Eun-hee to see a movie studio was at 2 a.m. When she said she would like to meet his sister, he ordered his aides to fetch her. It was gone 1 a.m.

For exercise, he swims. He also rides horses, claiming that he's been galloping eight kilometers a day at a speed of between 40 and 60 kilometers per hour since he was 11 years old.[11]

Kim Jong-il seeks the advice of his associates more than his father did, and makes decisions on the basis of discussion.[12] Like his father, he can be ruthless with political enemies or people who cross him, but can be more forgiving of small errors and moral lapses. While Kim Il-sung operated through his strong control of aides and officials, Kim Jong-il stresses organizational management. Defectors say Kim Jong-il tends to maintain formal relations with the heads of government ministries and offices, while more frequently contacting their deputies. He prefers dealing with people individually rather than addressing groups. Interestingly, while reluctant to make public addresses, Jong-il is by all accounts a great talker in private meetings once he gets inspired.

His source of legitimacy — his father — is also his greatest obstacle. Jong-il palpably lacks both the charisma and the heroic resume of Kim Il-sung. This may to some extent explain Jong-il's secretive style, in that it allows him both to conceal his shortcomings and to come across as modest while, most importantly, maintaining the presence of his father's spirit in his own leadership. His rule is, in fact, characterized by the notion, "The Great Leader is always with us."

As an absolute leader, Kim Jong-il needs to be careful to avoid being associated with failure. In 1996, at the height of the famine, he indicated in speeches that economic management was the responsibility of other officials. But then, in a conversation with visiting Korean-Japanese in 1998, he demonstrated that he was clearly in charge. He noted, for example, that while the Chinese would buy foreign power plants because their own equipment was inferior, North Koreans had been buying partial plants from overseas and completing them with locally sourced parts. "As a result, the plants we have bought this way have turned out to be worthless," he complained. "Look at the Pyongyang Thermal Power Plant. Its equipment was supplied by the Soviets... With a generator broken, Pyongyang citizens are now shivering with cold. I cannot stand it. So, when we find oil in our country, I plan to have all the existing thermal power plants demolished and build oil-fueled ones to replace them."[13]

Business people from the South Korean Hyundai conglomerate, who have held extensive talks with Kim Jong-il on joint economic projects, report that he is indeed very hands-on in economic matters. He had wanted them to invest in a proposed free economic zone around the town of Sinuiju on the Chinese border, but after reading a Hyundai feasibility study that concluded it would not be commercially viable, agreed to their proposal for a zone in Kaesong, near the DMZ. He complained to the South Koreans that his own economic officials lacked a grasp of capitalism, admitting that the North Koreans mistrusted proposals by visiting western bankers because they didn't understand what they were talking about. The impression the South Koreans have is of an engaged leader, more educated than his father, and more aware of the ways in which his country lags behind the South.

Perhaps the most recent testament to an active nature comes from a man who accompanied Kim Jong-il on his much-publicized 24-day train trip through Russia in the summer of 2001.

In a book called *Orient Express*, Konstantin Pulikovskiy, the Russian president's special representative to the country's Far Eastern Federal District, describes the North Korean leader's "powerful aura" and "strong energy." Pulikovskiy was surprised by Kim Jong-il's knowledge of Russia. Traveling through one region, the Dear Leader began asking Pulikovskiy detailed questions about the area. His questions "clearly indicated that he knew virtually everything about the situation."[14] For example, Kim Jong-il reportedly asked why the region's former governor had been transferred. Some of his knowledge came by way of one of two large suspended screens in his carriage which featured an electronic map providing satellite information on the regions they passed through.

(The second screen was apparently for showing movies. Kim Jong-il's interest in movies is well known. Shin Sang-ok, the kidnapped South Korean movie producer, said Kim Jong-il had a library of 15,000 movies when he was there in the mid-1980s. This may now have grown to 20,000, the figure Pulikovskiy cites in 2001, based on comments made to him by Russian President Vladimir Putin.)

As mentioned earlier, Kim Jong-il likes to party. Defectors have reported that he has a "Joy Brigade" of female entertainers, whose members are allegedly scouted from high schools each summer. To qualify for this dubious honor, the girls must be virgins. There were also reports in the 1980s that Kim hired "dancers" from Sweden and Russia to liven up his parties. There is one episode in which he ordered five dancing girls to strip naked and then instructed officials at the party to dance with them, but warned, "Don't touch."[15] Despite this, there are no consistent reports to suggest that the North Korean leader is particularly debauched, at least no more so than your average businessman in Asia.

Indeed, the don't-touch instruction may even suggest he is a tad prudish. There is a story that after an aide who took care of his official residence confided to the Dear Leader that he had had sex in all of Kim Jong-il's five cars, the Dear Leader responded by having the vehicles burned.[16]

Kim Jong-il's relaxed approach, even in formal situations, is one of his trademarks. During the televised inter-Korea summit of 2000, it became clear that he can chat and laugh quite freely. In Moscow in 2001, Putin invited him to his Kremlin apartment for lunch. The impromptu invitation, to coincide with the Kim train coming back through Moscow from St. Petersburg, reportedly changed the nature of the relationship between the two men. "It was a simple, home-cooked meal," Pulikovskiy writes. "Before that, [Kim] had seemed somewhat reluctant to show his emotions. After Moscow, however, he was more open, trusting and genial."

Putin reportedly found him educated and intelligent, with a good hold of international affairs and a sense of humor. Of the meetings, Kim said, "If people act like diplomats when they are with me, I also become a diplomat. Putin was honest with me, however, and I bared my soul to him."

Of course, there are times when he can be most undiplomatic. A senior Iranian official went to visit Kim Jong-il once. The foreign visitor spoke for about 10 minutes, after which Kim Jong-il said, "Is that all? Goodbye."[17]

What should we make of these contradictory episodes? Do they suggest that Kim's political character is positive or negative? This is a crucial question.

One problem with active–negative personalities, says Barber, is that they tend to invest everything in the outcome of one policy, which they doggedly refuse to adjust, even in the face of overwhelming pressure and sound advice. Barber cites Lyndon

Johnson's escalation of the Vietnam War as an example. In Kim Jong-il's case, would it be his dogged pursuit of Communism in the face of famine and collapse? Actually, not. Changing an entire political system is not a matter of policy choice. This is only likely to happen with a change of regime. However, we could make the case that his dogged pursuit of nuclear weapons derives from a negative personality. Kim has had a hard time making his mark on North Korean history. Somewhere in the back of his mind, he must know the odds on him becoming known as the leader whose removal marks the end of the communist state and the beginnings of a unified Korea are pretty high. While his country is walking the plank of failure, perhaps he feels he can bully the world into not pushing him to the edge. If the Dear Leader feels that nuclear weapons are key to his survival and if he is a negative personality, he might sink his teeth into this one like a pit bull and not let go until he is blasted out of his bunker.

On the other hand, if he is a positive character, he will be looking for a different kind of survival and will exhibit flexibility in its pursuit.

In making our judgment, how can we tell if he is positive or negative? The positive character exhibits an ability to laugh at himself, has a measure of self-esteem, and would exhibit flexibility in policy. If he were a negative character, we could expect to see evidence of depression, frustration, a chip on the shoulder, complaints of powerlessness, of being trapped by obligation. Meanwhile, we don't want to rush to misdiagnose his qualities or be distracted by the irrelevant. For example, his bouffant hairstyle and the revelation that he wears platform shoes have been cited as evidence of an inferiority complex. But what's wrong with wanting to add a couple of inches at both ends?

My broad sense of Kim Jong-il's personal character is that for a long time he struggled with negativity, having lost his mother and spent his hormone years in a blended family. The story of his childhood remains unclear, but no doubt the death of his brother and his mother by the time he was seven would have had a profound effect. While there is no solid account of his relationship with his stepmother, we suspect that relations were strained. We do know that in his twenties, Kim Jong-il battled with his uncle, Kim Yong-ju, who was considered a possible successor to Kim Il-sung, although it is not clear how serious and emotional this struggle was. He probably also suffered, as we've suggested, from a feeling that he was rather small and unattractive to women. None of these, on their own, suggest that he is necessarily rotten.

As we've seen, Kim Jong-il was said to have been rather wild and was probably cocky and rude to his teachers. While this behavior could be attributed to deep hurt, it is possible that it arose from elitism. From an early age, as the son of the Great Leader, Jong-il must have become accustomed to the shrinking deference of those around him. He probably learned early on that he was safe in an environment that was very dangerous for everyone else. He must have known of people who disappeared in the middle of the night or who were cast out by a single, small mistake and the twitch of his father's eyebrow. Jong-il grew up to understand that the underlying determinant of right and wrong in North Korea was loyalty to his father. This was the law by which North Koreans had to live and he was insensitive to the fate of those who broke it.

By all accounts, Kim Jong-il has something of a temper. "When he is happy, he can treat you really, really well. But when he is angry he can make every window in the house shake," his former sister-in-law, Sung Hae-rang, told *Time* in 2003.[18] "He has a personality of extremes, all colliding within the same mind." When he loses interest in people or turns against them, their careers and even their lives are in danger, she said. One defector claimed that when a subordinate asked how long Kim Il-sung would live, Kim Jong-il ordered the man executed.[19]

Just as emotions are more freely expressed among family members, so the "son-turned-father of the people" has no need to exhibit restraint with his extended family of aides and officials. "If subordinates misbrief him or commit a mistake, he throws things, even at top-ranking officials," his former Japanese chef, Kenji Fujimoto, told the Japanese daily *Sankei Shimbun* after publishing a book of his experiences.[20] He is on his best behavior with visitors, but even then it can sometimes be hard to reign himself in. Officials of the South Korean Daewoo conglomerate say Kim Jong-il became furious with its founder, Kim Woo-joong, when the two disagreed at a lunch in the early 1990s with Kim Il-sung. Father reportedly had to intervene to tell the Dear Son to cool it. "Among South Korean businessmen, Kim Woo-joong is the worst," he told Korean-Japanese visitors in 1998. "[He] is a very crafty wretch. He is literally two-faced."[21]

Tantrum throwing, of course, can be strategic. In the authoritarian Korean management culture, throwing a fit, rather than indicating a loss of control, is frequently used as a way of showing who's boss. This is beginning to change in South Korea as those with power increasingly need to work for the support of those they once lauded over: politicians need votes, managers need worker cooperation, and even presidential Blue House officials in Seoul, at this time of writing, are having to submit to a new performance assessment which requires input from subordinates. But, by Korean standards, the North is still a very old-fashioned place and the more authoritarian habits prevail.

A disturbing feature of Kim Jong-il's temper is that he reportedly appears to forget what he has said and thereby is somewhat disengaged from the consequences. For example, when he found out that his first son, Jong-nam, had a girlfriend, in his fury he instructed that food be cut off to the house in which Jong-nam lived with his mother and aunt. Two months later, he called to reprimand them for not having put in their regular order for food shipments.[22]

Perhaps he just forgot what he'd said in the heat of the moment. Other instances of forgetfulness can have far-reaching consequences. In 1996, Kim Jong-il was in the North Korean city of Wonsan when he noticed a group of boys aged around ten years old in the street. He made some comment about their straggly hair. Aides over-interpreted this as an instruction and an order went out through the country that young boys' heads be shaved. Two years later, in a discussion an official reminded him of his "instruction". He didn't remember having said it.[23]

Kim Jong-il can also present a kinder, gentler side. His sister-in-law portrayed an involved family man — even if it is with three families. She described how he would patiently walk up and down with the infant Jong-nam on his back till he fell asleep.[24] Another time, his sister-in-law recalled, he came home distraught from a hunting trip. He had shot a pregnant deer and had it taken to the hospital, where the baby fawn was put in an incubator. She also said he takes an interest in other people. "He'll ask you about yourself, about your thoughts and opinions," she told *Time*. "He has a talent for making people feel at ease when he wants to."

He does this sometimes through humor, and particularly at his own expense, an indication of the "positive" political personality. The before-mentioned comment about his horns or lack thereof indicates a relaxed awareness of how he is perceived in the outside world. When he met then-US Secretary of State Madeleine Albright in 2000, he referred to himself as the last of the "communist devils."[25]

Even funnier was a joke he made on himself in order to break the ice with Choi Eun-hee after his goons brought her to North Korea. The first time she sat down to dinner with him, he could see that she was nervous.

"Madame Choi, how do I look?" he asked, eyeing himself mockingly from one side and then the other. "Don't you think that I look like a midget's turd?" Choi and the other officials present laughed.[26]

Kim Jong-il's style of speech has inspired analysis in South Korea. Based on a conversation with him which Shin and Choi secretly taped in 1983, and also on a 1998 conversation with leaders of Chosen Soren, the association of pro-Pyongyang Koreans in Japan, he comes across to South Koreans as a big talker, slightly frivolous and with a tendency to say things he shouldn't. He takes off on flights of fancy and frequently changes subjects, but despite this lack of focus, he gets his point across. Analysis of these tapes has led Lee Kun-hu, a psychologist for South Korea's intelligence organization, to conclude that Kim is "a person with a light-hearted personality."[27] Dr Lee believes that Kim Jong-il is more of an artist than a statesman.

> By inborn nature, Kim Jong-il is highly susceptible and passionate and tends to have the characteristics of an artist not bound by rules. By acquired nature, he carried the traits of control, elaborateness, calculation, and reason, the traits he acquired in the course of controlling himself in the effort to secure and safeguard his role in the social system. But, a strong peculiarity as expressed outwardly is the sensitive faculty. It may well be said that his character is strong in a sentimental aspect and weak in reason... Kim Jong-il's showmanship or sense of humor seems inborn.[28]

Dr Lee observed that a "sentimental person" tends to set the atmosphere when meeting a "logical person" and that the former has more general public appeal, which would explain the strong, positive impression Kim Jong-il made on the South Korean public during the 2000 summit meeting with the dour, rational Kim Dae-jung.

In some regard, his artistic style makes Kim Jong-il quite refreshing, as if he is just an ordinary guy in power, rather than the smooth-talking advocate. For example, when asked by the South Korean publishers whether he and Kim Dae-jung had discussed revision of the South's national security laws, a longtime issue for the North, and of the section of the (North) Korean Workers' Party charter that calls for the overthrow of the South, he did not defend his own and criticize the other, as you would expect a politician to do.

> No, the revision of security laws in the South is up to South Korea. The charter of the Workers' Party has been revised in the past but the platform has remained unchanged since it was [adopted] in 1945. The platform contains several belligerent expressions as it was [written] back in the 1940s when Korea was liberated [from Japanese rule]. Among the top officials of the Workers' Party, there are several who have worked with President Kim Il-sung so I find [it] difficult to revise the platform. If the platform is changed, a lot of officials present here will have to quit their posts. Some may claim that if I initiate the revision of the platform, I am trying to purge my opponents.[29]

What kind of response is this? A subtle rejection of the idea? An explanation? An excuse? Kim Jong-il has the unpolitical manner — and the luxurious lifestyle — of a Hollywood movie star. His manner is not that of a politician or diplomat. Such lack of political deftness is distinctly un-Korean. His niece, Lee Nam-ok, who escaped from North Korea in 1992, has said that, compared with his "all-out Confucian" father, Kim Jong-il "in his personality has something like West European individualism or a trait of being very liberal."[30]

The kidnapped South Korean movie couple, Choi Eun-hee and Shin Sang-ok, saw first-hand that Kim Jong-il was not always taken in by the personality cult. On one occasion, the young women on a movie set started squealing with delight when Kim turned up. He turned to Shin and said, "It's fake." Shin's impression was that the North Korean leader conveyed a mixture of embarrassment and pride at his fans' behavior, but that at the same time was not fooled by it.

Such a reaction surprises us because we assume that the son of Kim Il-sung drinks in the adulation of the unwashed masses.

It is clear that Kim Jong-il does not have the same following as his father. Not only is he different from his father, but the country has also changed. East European reporters recall that, in the 1970s, when North Korean citizens placed bouquets at the foot of the Kim Il-sung statue on the occasion of his birthday, many would be in tears. At that time, the personality cult had worked on a generation since the Korean War, the country had slowly been developing, albeit at a slower pace than the South, and the leader was a genuine patriot with whose suffering they identified. By the late 1980s, however, the atmosphere on April 15, the Great Leader's birthday, was different. By then, the day had become more like a regular holiday and putting the flowers down was a kind of tradition. What had transpired in between was the emergence of Kim Jong-il as the successor. He is a far less sympathetic figure, as is clear from many of the defectors in Seoul, who are all negative about him, although they are less critical of Kim Il-sung.

Kim Jong-il must be aware of this difference, even if it's not discussed. He would, as any Korean, also be very aware that enthusiastic approval, while flattering, is essentially a self-advancement tactic on the part of its practitioners — if not a survival tactic, considering the penalties for perceived disloyalty.

To return to our search for "positive" or "negative" elements in Kim Jong-il's political make-up, an unexpected quality he appears to have is flexibility with policies. As mentioned, he indicated flexibility in his dealings with Hyundai. This suggests that his prime objective was to have the South Korean conglomerate involved, rather than have his own way in how they did it. Similarly, he listened closely to the advice of Shin Sang-ok about movie-making and immediately accepted and implemented many of his suggestions. Again, this indicates that his objective was for North Korea to make good movies and to have Shin involved, rather than to insist on his own way. This apparent flexibility is an important indication of positivity and would suggest that he has an ability to recognize mistakes and change tack to achieve results. (Within a certain framework, of course. As we have noted, Kim Jong-il is not going to turn his country capitalist overnight for it would undermine the legitimacy he draws from his father's rule.)

Even further, Kim Jong-il exudes a rather remarkable characteristic for a politician. He apologizes. He apologized to Shin and Choi for their suffering and said that those involved in the kidnapping — including himself — had undergone "self criticism" for how it was handled. On his train trip through Russia in 2001, he told Pulikovskiy that he'd heard Russian soldiers were heavy drinkers, and then apologized when he realized that his comment had been taken as a criticism. In a rather extraordinary sequence of events over a few weeks in 2002, he apologized to South Korea for a clash at sea provoked by the North Korean navy, and then admitted to and apologized to visiting Japanese Prime Minister Junichiro Koizumi for the kidnapping several years earlier of several Japanese citizens. And when in October 2002 his officials were confronted by the United States with evidence of his clandestine nuclear program, instead of having them deny, lie, accuse and throw tantrums, he told them to admit to it.

These examples may seem questionable from a moral perspective because, in fact, the right thing to do would be for the Dear Leader to turn himself in to the international court in The Hague for his crimes. Even politically, these apologies seem curious. For example, the apology to Koizumi appears to have been rather unwise politically because the details of the kidnappings then inflamed anti-North Korean sentiment in Japan. While the cycle of repentance and forgiveness is essential for healthy relationships — in Christianity, for example, it is a core concept of spiritual growth — in politics, repentance tends to invite calls for punishment and reparations. But if these cases suggest a certain naiveté, from the perspective of political character, his ability to apologize strongly suggests that he has a positive nature. Of course, in each case, there was a certain manipulative objective: he wanted Shin's and Choi's cooperation; in apologizing to Koizumi, he wanted to improve relations with Japan and secure reparations; and so on. But, at the same time, his strategy for achieving these ends — the apology — indicates a certain psychological freedom. He could, after all, have done what any normal politician would have done in his bid to achieve his goals — blame others — but he didn't.

My money, then, is on Kim Jong-il as an "active–positive" leader. I see him as the "sentimental" personality described above by Lee Kun-hu, at ease with himself despite emotional struggles in his early years, and able to be flexible in policy.

But, we should ask, how does this square with the fact that his state is a serious violator of human rights and international standards of behavior? In his analysis, Lee Kun-hu concludes that, strictly speaking, North Korea is not run by Kim Jong-il.[31] There is a different dynamic at work. The country is run by an organization, and that organization responds to one man — Kim Jong-il — aggrandizing everything he says and does in order to justify its own existence.

In other words, Kim Jong-il as an individual is neither insane nor evil. But he benefits from being at the top of a system which, as we shall see, is both.

8

Country of the Lie

Kim Jong-il, lest we forget, is the leader of a communist state. As such, he shares a historical stage with a cast of characters, now mostly dead, who in the twentieth century seized the political high ground in many countries, and whose course of action, made in the name of justice and equality, unleashed terrible savagery. While religion has a lot to answer for, no single belief system can match for sheer scale the destructiveness of Communism. During an average human lifespan in a developed country, its faithful dispatched an estimated 100 million people, by war, prison camp, and artificial famine.[1]

Given this outcome, Communism's wide appeal in its day is quite strange. You'd think people would have seen what was coming. They didn't because, despite its intellectual packaging, Communism essentially appealed to emotion. The ideology grew out of the suffering of the working class during the industrialization period in western Europe, but the anger and resentment it enshrined was readily picked up across the globe — wherever, indeed, there was anger and resentment. Once converted, adherents were bound emotionally to the tenets of the communist faith.

Communism's basis was Marxism–Leninism, a philosophy of political action rooted in dialectical materialism. And herein lay the clues to its failure. At heart, dialectical materialism is a lie: materialism holds that there is no spirit, no God, just stuff. But human beings are not just stuff. They are idealistic, they get inspired — a lot of them got inspired by Marx and Lenin — they fall in love, they laugh, they cry, and they intuitively conceive of themselves as resultant, created from a process that they do not fully understand but which, lying just outside their grasp, informs the deepest moments of their lives. Furthermore, they are the center of their own universe. When you shut your eyes, your world goes dark. A political system that denies this unique value of the individual and treats you as an object can only be sustained by a dictatorial elite. It can only work through suppression, injustice, and inequality. According to the other core element of communist thought, the dialectic, progress comes through conflict. But this makes as much sense as saying that babies can only be conceived through rape. While progress may require struggle and the overcoming of obstacles, it is also achieved through cooperation, even if that cooperation involves, as Victorian mothers told their daughters, just shutting your eyes and thinking of England.

Despite its conceptual flaws, Communism succeeded in attracting committed followers — the first generation in each revolution were often the most idealistic and self-sacrificial political activists — because the lie was obscured by a half-truth. It attacked current injustices, which could not be denied, and promised to resolve them and create an ideal society. But a spirit of hatred manifested in its strategy: utopia required the elimination of identified human obstacles in the way: the middle class, religious believers, landowners, non-communists. The fear generated by such a process fed on itself and communist states became characterized by the dialectic's endless need for enemies, within or without. Through suppression and propaganda, it throttled the joy out of the societies it ran.

Being materialist, Communism could not postpone heaven to

the afterlife, and after a generation it became apparent that the ideal society was a fiction. What also became apparent was that the non-materialist societies of the West were providing better material comfort for their people. They were also democratic. This recognition was Communism's undoing. The inevitable emergence from Communism, country by country, depended on the underlying culture; but 80 years after the 1917 Russian revolution, most communist states had moved on.

Former US President Ronald Reagan's much-mocked reference to the Soviet Union as the "evil empire" was profoundly to the point: like Nazism, Communism was an evil ideology not because it made people evil but precisely because it required or at least encouraged otherwise good people to take monumentally inhumane action.

North Korea's communists began as Marxist-Leninists fighting to free their country from Japanese imperialist rule. Kim Il-sung later introduced his *Juche* (self-reliance) amendment. This political thought represented an end to his dependence on Moscow and Beijing and proposed a flexible application of Marxism–Leninism to the particular circumstances of Korea. But far from a move into pragmatism, as you would think, *Juche* actually provided philosophical underpinning to the personality cult.

Man is the master of his fate, says *Juche*, and the master of the revolution is the people, and the Korean communist revolution must be pursued self-reliantly. (This last point explains North Korea's isolation and disengagement from international norms, such as, for example, the way its diplomats in some countries peddle drugs).[2] Key to *Juche* is the role of the *suryong*, the supreme leader. For the revolution to succeed, all must line up in thought and action behind him.

Cutting through the verbiage — and *Juche* texts will strike the reader as turgid to the point of being devoid of sense — *Juche* is designed to bend Communism and everything else to the cause of one man, the Leader.

North Korea claims to be a "workers' paradise," but in fact everything about it manifests an underlying hatred of human beings. Schoolchildren learn math by adding and subtracting numbers of dead American soldiers.[3] A Korean phrase book I bought in the hotel in Pyongyang explains verb tenses with the examples, "We fight against Yankees, We fought against Yankees, We will fight against Yankees." It explains Korean sentence structure with the example, "Yankees are wolves in human shape," which in Korean word order comes out as, "Yankees in human shape wolves are." Among useful phrases in the "On the Way to the Hotel" section is, "Let's mutilate US imperialism!"

In this hateful state, there is a great deal of anger. One surprising thing about North Korea, surprising because you expect robots, is how heavily the men drink and how frequently fights break out. "I saw soldiers attack one another with broken glass," said Norbert Vollertsen, a doctor with the Cap Anamur aid agency, who was in the country in 1999 and 2000. "In hospital, I saw many such victims."[4] No wonder Kim Jong-il instructed his guards to be polite to each other.

Another feature of North Korea is suspicion of outsiders. All foreigners are suspect. One afternoon on my first trip in 1989, there was a knock on my hotel room door and there stood a Russian reporter with whom I had become friendly over the years covering stories in the truce village of Panmunjom. Normally an effusive man, he stood there silently with a finger to his lips. He beckoned me to follow him. We walked along the corridor, took an elevator, and walked out onto a roof garden, all without speaking. Then, in the open air, he turned with a huge smile and threw his arms around me, breaking silence in a heavy accent, "Michael, it is wonderful to see you here! Be careful of the bugs in the room!"

A Bulgarian diplomat advised me to check the mirrors. "If there's a mirror which you can't see behind, they might even be filming you," he warned. Indeed, there was a large, full-length mirror set into the wall. My roommate, a Scotsman I'll call Bob because he might not get a visa again if I expose him, and I started having long, loud conversations about how splendid North Korea was and how we felt it our mission to educate the world about this jewel of the northeast. One of these started after Bob had taken a shower. A stocky, hairy fellow, he came out of the bathroom with a towel around his waist and positioned himself with his back to the large mirror. Still singing the praises of the Great and Dear leaders, he let the towel drop and bent over, presenting our imagined camera team with a startlingly close up view of his parted buttocks. This test of the security system was repeated over several days, and we experienced no adverse reaction from hotel staff. Having "swept" our room thus, we judged it to be free of cameras at least.

The phone bugs were another matter. One afternoon my guide told me, "You know, we consider the Swedes to be enemies." That lunchtime, I had called a Swedish diplomat from the room and made arrangements to meet him the next day in the hotel coffee shop. On another trip, the photographer in our group sat up through the night for a week on an open international line trying to electronically file each day's photographs. On the last day, our complaints must have reached the right person because the line was miraculously cleared.

Foreign diplomats, of course, have lived with such stories for decades. A Russian living in a foreigners' apartment in the 1990s drank heavily at a dinner party and started cursing the two Kims. The others pointed at the ceiling with desperate gestures to get him to shut up. "To hell with the bastards," he slurred. "So what if they hear? What can they do? Turn off the electricity?" Sure enough, a few minutes later, they did. The oddest story I have heard was of two Danish engineers, in North Korea for a few months on a project, who complained in their hotel room one night about how boring it all was. "If I'd known, I would have brought a pack of cards with me," one said. The next day at work, their guide presented them with a pack of cards. The unusual part of this story was that they had been talking in Danish. A Czech-speaking defector later told me that language students were brought to the hotels to tune in to visitors.

And so the stories go.

If there's a consistent theme that comes through in any dealings with North Korea, it is lack of truthfulness. The lack of light at night is highly symbolic. North Korea is truly a country of darkness, in the grip of a massive lie that its highest leaders have a stake in preserving, that even the elite and the knowing are fearful of challenging, that many more just have to find a way to live with, and that the many innocent swallow whole. This is a country whose future course necessitates cutting through the lies that bind it.

Pyongyang, the capital, is itself a big lie. Its boulevards and magnificent buildings present a stirring but misleading panorama. The first-time visitor may be impressed to a point, but it doesn't take long for the absence of traffic and commerce — it must be the only city in the world where the main noise on downtown streets is the footfall of pedestrians — to generate a nagging feeling of unreality. Pyongyang is too perfect, and its people are not representative. Over the years, undesirable elements, such as the handicapped, the elderly, bicycles, and animals, have been moved to the provinces. The cheerlessness even of those lucky ones who remain presents a marked contrast to the energy and decibel level of their brethren in the South.

Predictably, the guides — and you have to have one — will fib when you ask difficult questions. Much of the lying is mundanely mystifying. Once a foreign resident said we could use her car to go with our guides to Keumgang Mountain for the weekend. She was not present herself to supervise this arrangement, which got overruled by someone. We were kept waiting for an entire morning in the hotel lobby without explanation and then told we had to pay several hundred dollars for two official cars, one for us and one for the guides. Would it have been so hard to tell us why we were not permitted to use our friend's car, whatever the truth was?

Actually, it might have been. Visitors to North Korea who get irritated with the spin-doctoring and lack of explanations assume a conspiracy. But it is likely that the guides themselves do not have the full picture. They may be confused. Indeed, North Koreans exposed to the outside world are often very confused. One highly educated North Korean I had befriended in China once confided his confusion to me.

"Mr Breen, I have something important I would like to talk about," he started. We were walking along a Chinese street, away from possible bugs or eavesdroppers.

"Oh?" I thought he was going to ask me to help him defect.

"Yes. Since I have been here I have been reading the foreign press. According to everything that I have been taught, what foreign reporters say about North Korea is wrong. But when I read the articles, I cannot see where they are wrong." This rare glimpse into one individual's struggle moved me profoundly because, in revealing it, he was trusting me with his life. Had I been a North Korean citizen, even hearing his confession of confusion would have put me at risk. I am ashamed to say, though, that I was also moved by selfish relief that he wasn't asking for help to defect. At the time, I had left journalism and was a consultant dealing with western companies interested in North Korea. I could not have refused a request to help someone defect, but it would have ended my business. This instant mixture of warm trust, self-interest, panic, and sudden relief gave me a glimpse into the fearful life of North Koreans.

Such is life when fear underlies every public interaction. In this paranoid state, every foreigner is a potential CIA agent plotting to assassinate the leader. The North Korean student studying Czech language once met a Czech diplomat in a public park to discuss some arrangements for a state-sanctioned visit to

Prague, and was interrogated for five hours afterwards by security officials wanting to know everything that was said.

As a foreign visitor, after a few days, when the novelty of being in *1984* has worn off, the lie starts to wear you down. It helps to have a funny man in your team, like Bob. He was a photographer and had that brand of humor that goes with the profession. As I engaged guides in conversation to get quotes for my stories, Bob would listen for a while and, when he'd had enough, start humming the theme to "The Twilight Zone." On another occasion, when we were in a rare shop for tourists, he came upon two bottles of liquor, each containing a dead snake. One was bigger than the other. "Look," he said after observing them for a moment. "The Great Snake and the Dear Snake."

One time, though, even he lost it. We were being taken around the Pyongyang Students and Children's Palace, where little kids learn the arts, and play instruments, and sing cutesy songs about the Dear Leader for visitors. Bob disappeared. We found him later sitting in the van in a foul mood. "The bastards," he fumed. Himself the father of a young daughter, the spectacle of innocence strapped to the cause of the regime infuriated him so profoundly that he removed himself rather than risk a public explosion of Scottish temper.

Information control is crucial to maintaining the lie. One consequence of this practice is a serious gap in knowledge. Occasionally, these combine with the earnestness of its promoters in a laughable way. One such moment was in 1995, when a group of American and Japanese wrestlers arrived to perform in a two-day event that was treated like the Olympics. Clearly, this was an event that was micro-managed at the highest levels. The force behind it was a Japanese wrestler-turned-politician who had been trained by a North Korean master and wished to honor him by staging the tournament. Such humble acknowledgement by a representative of the beastly Japanese of the superiority of North Korea opened all doors. Among the VIPs invited for the occasion was Mohammed Ali. The hosts, ignorant to news of the outside world, did not know until he arrived that his Parkinson's disease made even speech difficult.

On the first night, the masses filled the 150,000-seat stadium. The wrestling ring was in the center of the pitch and, as foreigners, we had front row seats. The wrestlers made typically grand entrances. One was a Japanese woman with a three foot-high pile of blue hair. The North Korean crowd did not quite know what to make of this. My favorite wrestler, who provided my most thrilling moment in North Korea and one which I wish could have been beamed to the world, was an African-American who arrived to the accompaniment of very loud, pulsating music, wearing a Stars and Stripes gown and high-fiving his way down a gauntlet of foreigners on the pitch. He leapt into the ring, hurled off the gown, did some funky gyrations and then jumped up on the ropes. From this position, he gripped an imaginary rifle and swiveled round to point it at the royal box, in which Party Secretary Kim Yong-soon and others were sitting (the Dear Leader must have been watching on TV at home), as if to say, "Hi!" This flourish was timed with the dramatic final beat of the music. The open-mouthed silence of 150,000 North Koreans swallowed the whoops of the handful of foreign WWF fans.

By the second day, the North Koreans realized that pro-wrestling is entertainment, not a sport, and that they should not have taken it so seriously. Seeing it live in North Korea was a true experience of weird meets weird.

It is worth noting that what we know of North Korea comes largely by way of translation. South Koreans find the North's propaganda weird enough, but in English it is doubly so for simple reasons of style. In Korean, for example, long sentences and repetition of words do not sound awkward in the way they do in English. North Korea has long employed a team of foreign copy-editors for English, French, Spanish, and Arabic translations, who have had their own struggles. Two were jailed in the 1960s.[5] A Brit, Andrew Holloway, wrote at length about his experiences in the late 1980s.[6] Jean-Jacques Grauhar, a young Frenchman, spent seven years in Pyongyang as a copy-editor and later as a business consultant.[7] Michael Harrold, a Brit who held out for six years as the English proofreader, once regaled visitors in a bar in Pyongyang with some of the challenges of the job. "I got one across my desk today: 'the Yankee soldiers took out their bayonets and sliced through the women's breasts like bean curd,'" he said. "Now what the hell do I do with that?"

Still, foreigners can always leave (with a few kidnapped exceptions). Not so the locals. Even expressing a desire to leave could land them in a concentration camp. The enemy within is usually the object of more virulent hatred, as evidenced by the innocents suffering in the country's gulag. And, for communists, this enemy is always lurking inside the gate. "As the history of the international communist movement shows," Kim Jong-il wrote in a North Korean magazine, "all the ideological confusion and all the twists and turns within it are due to the fact that renegades of the revolution have appeared in its upper strata."[8]

The irony, though, is that the article that this quote comes from was probably itself a lie. We may assume that Kim Jong-il himself believes in some of the revolution rubbish, but surely he knows that much of it is also nonsense.

One day, the Dear Leader was watching propaganda shots of smiling children on television when his sister-in-law, Sung Hae-rang, commented on how forced it was and asked if he couldn't do something about it.

"I know," the all-powerful dictator said wearily. "But if I tell them to tone down the artificiality, they will go completely in the opposite direction and find the most dirty, wretched children they can, dressed in horrible rags."[9]

So, he knows.

His artistic, somewhat unconventional side knows the truth of North Korea, but he lacks the will, originality, effort, and possibly the means, to make his an honest state. And as we noted in the previous chapter, to act to change the system would be his undoing.

It's ironic to hear, though, that he hates untruthfulness. While his people live a lie, he, like the interrogator in the camp, insists on being told the truth. "He hates — positively hates — liars," Sung told *Time*. "This is the thing that angers him like nothing else."

You wonder then how he feels about his titles. There are a few whoppers there. He is most famously known as the Dear Leader, which is how school textbooks refer to him, but he's also at various times been called the Party Center, Unique Leader, Wise Leader, Respected Leader, Supreme Commander, Father of the People, Great Leader, Morning Star of Paekdu, Outstanding Military Strategist, Leader of Steel, Father of the Nation, Leader of the People, Our Father, Dear General, Great General, Our General, Leader of the Twenty-First Century, Sun of the Twenty-First Century, Glorious Sun of the Twenty-First Century, Son of Mt. Paekdu, Sun of Mankind, Everlasting Sky, and probably some we've missed.[10]

With its lies, its fear-mongering, its hatred, its self-absorption, and with its controls and with the confusion it sows, North Korea as a state has the hallmarks of an evil personality. In his book, *People of the Lie: The Hope for Healing Human Evil*, the psychotherapist Scott Peck identifies a key characteristic of evil people as being an "unsubmitted will." [11]

"All adults who are mentally healthy submit themselves one way or another to something higher than themselves, be it God or truth or love or some other ideal," Peck writes. "They believe in what is true rather than what they would like to be true." But, in his experience, patients who he believed to be clinically evil, on the other hand, do not submit in this way. If there was a struggle between their guilt and their will, will won. Evil people, he says, exhibit a determination to have their own way and will draw on greater reserves of power to control others. The failure to submit to God, conscience or an ideal outside of oneself is characteristic of a form of self-absorption known as "malignant narcissism," the term used by Jerrold M. Post in his analysis of Kim Jong-il's personality.[12] A democratic state submits to its constitution, to international law and norms, to regular free elections and allows commentators and critics free rein. That makes it good. That is as much as we can expect from a political system. The rest is up to society, religion, individuals, culture, business and so on. The politician's role in democratic states is to create the structure within which individuals can flourish and reach for the stars.

North Korea does the opposite. We may say that Kim Jong-il himself submitted to the will of his father, but the state appears "unsubmitted." It is thoroughly self-absorbed and exhibits an extraordinary will to survive and cause trouble. In exercising this will, it devours its own. Literally. Consider that in recent years, North Korea has lost 10 percent of its people to famine and has become an international beggar. And yet it acts as if its enemies should queue up for the privilege of donating to it. Given its mentality, if a leader like Kim Jong-il were to strengthen the rights of the individual, he would be seen by the faithful as weakening the power of the state on which the people depend. It would be a crime. Similarly, if economic reforms are introduced and wealth increases, individual thinking may spread and the need for the leader's fatherly guidance may diminish. Such weakening would be a crime against what they believe, which is in the power of the Leader.

And so the state is stuck.

North Koreans seem like good folk — innocent and good-hearted people. Perhaps this is because they, as individuals, have submitted to something outside of themselves. True, they have had no choice, and they submit to a lie and to a thuggish regime. But inasmuch as they are submitted, they are good. We should bear that in mind when we consider how horribly they have suffered.

CHAPTER

9

The Gulag

N orth Koreans are noted for their strange behavior. There is no end to the examples of the bizarre and seemingly irrational, from the returning POWs at the end of the Korean War who stripped naked as they were returned across the border, to the nutty propaganda — such as a claim that Kim Jong-il eagled and holed-in-one his way around the Pyongyang golf course — to the tearful citizens who meet their South Korean kin for the first time in 50 years and exclaim, "Thanks to the Dear Leader, we can see one another again."

Of course, there are explanations.

The POWs feared they would be suspected of having collaborated with their captors, so removed even the clothes the enemy had put them in. The propagandists fear punishment for lack of zeal. Those with South Korean relatives fear being reclassified as "hostile" after the officially arranged reunions.

Such fear is difficult to spot, let alone understand, if you come from a free country. But it explains so much. It explains why people walk silently in the streets of Pyongyang. It is the reason locals do not make friends with foreign residents. It explains why citizens turn away from foreigners who ask them directions. It explains why those dealing with foreigners exhibit no curiosity about the guests' countries. It's why officials ramble on ad nauseum about how wonderful the Dear Leader is when they probably know he's a freak. It explains why North Korean officials can be good guys over a beer and mindless when engaging in formal negotiations. It explains why the people who eavesdrop on you want you to know they're listening: they want to make you behave, because they risk punishment if you don't. Fear washes like a foul spew through the society, its bitterness tasted at even the highest levels.

Fear also numbs other emotions. It has a way of rendering its victims indifferent to others. In the winter of 2000, Norbert Vollertsen, the German doctor, was traveling north of Pyongyang when he saw a body in the road. "The driver and the guides didn't want to stop because they thought it would get them into trouble," he said.[1] When Vollertsen and a colleague yelled in protest and threatened to jump out of the moving car, the driver agreed to turn back. (Perhaps he feared worse trouble if he had to explain how he lost both foreign passengers.) They knelt to examine the body.

> The man was dead, but I faked an examination with a stethoscope to try and see how he had died. He was a uniformed soldier, probably around 20, but he had the arms of a 12-year-old. Malnutrition. I uncovered his back. My colleague had been a nurse in East Germany and was familiar with torture victims. She pointed out old and recent scars and cigarette burns. There was a large open wound on his back through which I could see bone.

When Vollertsen went to take a photograph, the driver and his guides pounced on him and seized the camera. Fear.

Dead bodies were presumably not an everyday occurrence, but yet these North Koreans lacked the sense of civic duty to report it, the curiosity to wonder what had happened, and the decency to take any action in consideration of the man's family. Goodness has retreated because North Koreans are afraid for themselves.

"Everyone in North Korea is afraid," I once said to a North Korean in Moscow. There was a pause of about three minutes.

"Tell me a secret about yourself," he said. Then it was my turn to pause. I told him of first-marriage struggles that I had not confided in anyone else. He then told me of a friend whose father had been put away on a corruption charge. Of itself, the case was unremarkable. What was unusual was being told about it. His tale and his trepidation at revealing it — and I should say that defectors in Seoul have cynically suggested that he was simply mining me for personal details — gave me at the time a sense of the overwhelming suffering of good and innocent people in a country gripped by a monstrous, malignant, narcissistic, and shockingly evil regime.

What all North Koreans know about and are afraid of is the gulag.

South Korean intelligence estimated in 1999 that there were over 200,000 prisoners in 10 sprawling camps in remote parts of the country. These were later merged into five after the locations were publicized in South Korean news reports. Prisoners are organized into what from the air look like ordinary villages. Some villages are for offenders with fixed terms and others are for lifers.

The gulag has been around from the start. Many survivors from the camps created by the communists when they took power in the late 1940s made it to South Korea during the Korean War. Over the years, I met some. One was a former underground anti-communist operative, another a Methodist pastor who survived a massacre by lying still in a mound of dead bodies. One man had been a North Korean army lieutenant and been given the cushy job of organizing prisoner work teams in the 1,500-man facility by the camp commandant, who by good fortune had gone to the same school. Another former prisoner had become a professor in Seoul, and another worked as an oriental medicine doctor. All these survivors told of a system that combined Japanese techniques of torture with Soviet use of inmates for labor. But their stories of violence, injustice, and hunger were lost in the muddle of Cold War priorities. As South Korea was itself such a violator of individual rights until the late 1980s, its attempts to expose North Korean crimes were often considered suspect.

Under the influence of Soviet advisors in the North Korean Interior Ministry in the late 1940s and 1950s, internal security campaigns focused on political opponents and "class enemies," such as religious believers and landlords. When these advisors were withdrawn in 1957, the Politburo in Pyongyang undertook a new form of purge.[2] In a process which really got going when Kim Il-sung's brother, Yong-ju, took charge, all citizens were investigated and classified as either "friendly," "neutral," or "hostile" on the basis of their family background. After trials in 1959, around 2,500 people were executed and 70,000 "hostiles" were relocated to remote mountain regions. In 1964, the citizenry was further divided into 51 sub-categories. Classification determined a citizen's prospects for marriage and career. It also determined the nature of punishment a person would receive if he or she got into trouble.

The international community first became aware of the North Korean prison system when two foreigners fell foul of it. Ali Lameda, a Venezuelan poet and a communist, and Jacques Emmanuel Sédillot, a Frenchman who had fought with the leftist International Brigade in Spain in the 1930s, worked in Pyongyang in 1966 as copy-editors, improving the Spanish and French translations, respectively, of Kim Il-sung's speeches and various publications. They were arrested after criticizing the propaganda, accused of being CIA spies, and sentenced to 20-year prison terms. Lameda was freed in 1974, after the Romanian leader, Nicolae Ceausescu, personally intervened. Sédillot died in North Korea, either in prison or shortly after his release.[3]

In the 1990s, a new generation of survivors, such as Kang Chol-hwan and Lee Soon-ok, and a former prison guard, Ahn Myong-chol, defected to South Korea and revealed the horrific picture of the modern North Korean gulag.[4] In 1998 and 2002, their evidence was presented at congressional hearings in Washington. Among their revelations was the story of a riot in 1987 at Onsung Prison in which 5,000 prisoners were massacred.

As in South Korea, Japan, and China, confession forms the basis for a case in North Korea, which means that torture is routine and confession to crimes not committed is commonplace. Lee Soon-ok was a Party member and supervisor in charge of a material distribution center in October 1986 when she was arrested after refusing to give a senior security official extra fabric to make a Kim Jong-il-style jacket. Her interrogation under a man named Kim Hak-nam began when she was thrown into a room of 20 or 30 men, covered with a blanket and punched and kicked by them until she blacked out. After this softening up, she was questioned for three days without being allowed to close her eyes. During several months of abuse, she was shoved into a brick kiln until she collapsed with the heat, strapped naked to a chair and flogged, fettered to a door, had her teeth punched out and sticks placed between her fingers and twisted.

"Sometimes the eyes of (Kim Hak-nam) and the inspection chief looked like those of ravenous animals, shining with an unearthly light," she wrote in her prison memoirs, published after she escaped from North Korea.[5]

One torment, which guards called the "frozen fish," was to make prisoners sit in their underclothes on their knees in the snow in sub-zero temperatures. Lee's feet and ears became frostbitten. On one occasion, she wrote, a guard in a warm dog-hair coat came outside and walked around a line of such prisoners, stamping his booted feet to keep warm. "Oh, it's so cold. I'm freezing to death," he said mockingly.[6]

Lee's worst experience came when she was strapped to a bench and had water forced into her mouth until she passed out. She awoke to find Kim Hak-nam and another man standing on a plank placed across her stomach. After this, she was unable to stand up for 15 days. By all accounts, this is standard treatment for anyone who tries to resist signing a confession. Suspects resist to avoid the punishment that goes with the "crime," especially if it involves a change in status that will impact the family. Ironically, some resist confessing because they have faith in the Party and think that the mistake of their arrest will be cleared up. Still resisting, Lee was moved to a second interrogation center where two groups of 12 guards, mostly junior officers in their twenties, worked shifts. The center consisted of 20 cells, 10 on either side of a walkway, each with a small back door that the inmate would have to crawl through like a dog. Prisoners were required to sit cross-legged, head-bowed and motionless, from 5 a.m. to 10 p.m. If they were seen moving, guards ordered them to put their hands out through the bars and then beat them with a truncheon.

In her memoirs, Lee gives a vivid account of other inmates she came across in the interrogation centers in 1986 and 1987. One was a man named Lee Yun-chel. A distribution manager, he was arrested after refusing to give televisions to some policemen. Under the frozen fish torture, his frostbitten ears swelled to the size of a child's hand and he became half paralyzed. Choi Young-hwan was a county commercial manager and a Korean War veteran. He gave a color TV set to a prosecutor, but was found out. The prosecutor, angry that his name was revealed and that he had to return the TV, later had Choi arrested. Choi's hands were burned in the kiln torture and became infected. He lost all feeling from his waist down and could not tell when he had urinated or defecated. He died in the interrogation center. The punishment didn't stop there. Because of his official reclassification as an offender, two of his sons were expelled from the army and a third kicked out of school; the family was moved to a farm commune and their assets confiscated. Kim Woong-kil, a provincial exporting official, had an ear cut off and died under torture. A 60-year-old fisheries official had committed no crime, but to satisfy his torturers concocted a story that he had stolen a whole train and sold it. A school principal who had discovered the bodies of two teachers in his school and called the police, was himself arrested for the murders. For protesting his innocence, he was given electric torture, which melted his ears and fingers. Some time later, when two thieves confessed to the murders, the principal, now lame and deformed, was released without an apology or compensation. He was, however, required to sign a document saying he would not reveal his experience.

Lee Soon-ok held out for a year, but then signed a confession when a new interrogator, Kim Chun-ho, threatened her family. After her trial, she spent the next five years in a prison in Kechon county. On her first day, a female officer kicked her in the chest and said, "You must give up being human if you want to survive here."[7]

Prison garb, second-hand and unwashed, was a pair of cotton pants, a cotton shirt and cotton socks. Newcomers were put in separate cells for a few days while they acclimatized. It had a small window, a hole for a toilet, a cabinet, a toothbrush, and powder toothpaste. There was a speaker for political broadcasts. On the wall were the regulations which prisoners had to learn before being transferred. These included an instruction to "adore the authorities of Kim Il-sung and Kim Jong-il with all your heart" and another forbidding chatter, laughter, and singing. When an officer summoned them, prisoners were required to "come quickly before him and sit on their knees."[8]

After a few days, Lee was moved into a large cell of 30 square meters where up to 90 women slept with their feet in one another's faces. A nine-meter high fence separated the women's section of the camp from the men's. The 6,000 prisoners in

Kechon were assigned to various departments and organized in work groups of five to seven. They worked 19-hour days, making coats, bags, belts, gun covers, dog muzzles, and other military items. Failure to meet quotas meant a reduction in the daily ration of 300 grams of corn and cabbage soup. Each night, two women in each cell were assigned to watch the others and report what they said in their sleep.

In 1988, inmates were put to work making bras for export to the Soviet Union and doilies for shipment to Poland.[9] Business went well and, in 1990, a new line was started knitting sweaters to be sent to Japan. Later, the prison received an order from France for paper roses. In 1992, prisoners slept at their machines for three months to meet the facility's quota of 10,000 student uniforms and 20,000 items of clothing being given free to citizens as a present from Kim Il-sung on his eightieth birthday. If a prisoner made a mistake, she was accused of damaging state property and her daily corn ration was reduced to 80 grams.

"If someone made a small spot on a product, she was beaten until she lost consciousness," Lee wrote. "If prisoners continuously made mistakes sewing doilies, they were placed in solitary confinement."

Among the other inmates Lee Soon-ok describes in her memoirs was a 39-year-old woman called Kim Young-hee, who had appealed to a higher court against a three-year sentence for stealing a kilo of sugar. The sentence was increased to 20 years. When another lady, Kim Jung-ok, explained to police why she had stolen a pack of corn to feed her hungry children, she was given 15 years for criticizing the government. Some inmates had committed real crimes. One young woman was serving 15 years for murdering her father. Kim Chun-hwa was put in solitary confinement for accidentally sewing a nail into a coat. The cell was so small that there was only room to sit. Spikes prevented prisoners from leaning against the walls. Kim's calf muscles stopped functioning and after release from the cell, she could not walk. She crawled. This pitiful sight invited beatings by female guards and one night, she died on the factory floor. Two prisoners were ordered to wrap the body in a blanket and take it away. An illiterate woman, Kim Young-sook, was beaten to death because a guard did not believe she couldn't read a knitting pattern. Suh Young-sun, a sweet and kind woman according to Lee, was a cook on a building site. She gave second helpings to the construction workers and, when they ran out of the month's rations early, she was accused of stealing government property and jailed. In 1989, when prisoners had to make costumes for the International Youth Festival, a communist event held in North Korea that year, Suh accidentally messed up one costume and hid it to avoid being punished. When the mistake was discovered, she was so afraid of being tortured that she agreed to whatever crime her interrogator accused her of. Having confessed to a capital offense, she was executed in front of all the prisoners in May 1990.

One spring, Lee writes, 150 prisoners became ill and died because the cooks did not have water to clean the cabbage. They were buried under a tree. The authorities wanted to keep the incident secret and the victim's families were not informed. In 1990, the ceiling of the plant where sweaters were made for export collapsed on some 20 prisoners, killing several. On another occasion, guards gathered the male prisoners and announced that whoever could get over the fence would be free. Many ran for the fence and were electrocuted. The officers laughed. A woman called Choi Sul-rung had lived in China. After a guard overheard her say she regretted having left, she was publicly executed for betraying the Party. In August 1988, prisoners were summoned to witness the execution of a male prisoner. One of the women recognized the man being tied to the post. It was her son. She did not know he was in the prison. She screamed and ripped out her own eyeballs so that she would not see him being shot. For this outburst, she too was executed.

Some women arrived pregnant. Poison was injected into the fetus, but some live babies were born. Prisoners assigned as medical assistants were ordered to strangle them. Kim Bung-ok gave birth to a boy and begged the medical officer not to kill him. The baby was throttled. The commotion attracted the attention of the senior medical officer and Kim was thrashed and put in the solitary cell where, five days later, she died.

"I thought that studying medicine would allow me to save people's lives," Kim Shin-ok, a prisoner in the medical department told Lee. "But look at me! I'm using my knowledge to hurt people." Kim believed that she would not be allowed to leave after her sentence was up because she had killed too many people and knew that the dead babies were used for "medical purposes."[10]

If they broke regulations, prisoners were sent to the "discipline department." One woman was sent for laughing, another for gazing at her reflection in a window. This department took care of the dirtiest jobs, such as cleaning out the pigsty and transferring human waste into a large tank for use as fertilizer. Few survived it.

Around 100 women in Kechon were religious believers serving 10-year sentences for "superstition." They were isolated from other prisoners, received less rations, and were subject to greater abuse because guards could receive promotions if they succeeded in making them recant. They were assigned to dangerous jobs, such as in the rubber factory, the smelting works, and the discipline department. Mostly elderly, they were paraded every month in front of the other prisoners and told that they would be given lighter jobs, and even released, if they denied their faith. On one murderous occasion, a Christian man was hung upside down and ordered to deny his beliefs. The prison warden became so enraged by his silence that he began to stab at the man with a stick. He was let down and beaten, but still said nothing. The warden stomped on him and then ordered the assembly of 6,000 prisoners to walk over him. In this way, he was trampled to death.

During the rainy season in the summer of 1991, a Christian woman working in the discipline department named Lee Ok-dan accidentally slipped into the sewage tank. It was so deep that they would have needed a rope to get her out. A guard told them to leave her to die. In a remarkable act of self-sacrifice, another Christian lady ignored the guard and climbed in to help her, followed by two more. The guard ordered the door of the tank closed and the four women died from the noxious fumes. The bodies were never taken out. The following year, in the smelting works, an officer ordered prisoners to pour molten iron on eight Christian men who had infuriated him by remaining silent when he ordered them to deny the existence of heaven.

Each year, prisoners were ordered to memorize Kim Il-sung's New Year speech. A mammoth mental effort — the speech would cover two full pages of a newspaper — older inmates just had to remember the contents, while younger prisoners were supposed to have learned it word for word by the time the Great Leader's April 15 birthday came around. Prisoners picked at random who couldn't remember it all were placed in solitary. When ordered to recite it, a male banker from Pyongyang protested, "I can die, but I cannot memorize the speech!" This was taken as an insult to the Great Leader and the man was publicly executed.

There are also children in the gulag, a result of Kim Il-sung's instruction that the seed of opposition to the revolution should be stamped out for three generations. Kang Chol-hwan was nine years old in 1977 when he was sent with his family to Yodok Prison after his grandfather, a businessman who had returned to North Korea from Japan and who was too vocal with his criticism of the government, was sentenced to a labor camp. Yodok was a sprawling facility built in a valley in 1974. Kang lived in a hut with his grandmother, his father, uncle and seven-year-old sister, Mi-ho. Grandfather, they later learned, was in a camp called

Senghori where offenders were put to work in coal mines. Kang's mother was forced to divorce his father and so avoided prison. In Yodok, the family lived in an earthen hut in a "village" of between 2,000 and 3,000 former residents of Japan and their families.

In his superbly written biography, *The Aquariums of Pyongyang,* Kang, who is now a reporter in Seoul for the daily *Chosun Ilbo,* reveals how hard it was at first for his communist grandmother to accept that the system was at fault:

> When we first arrived at the camp, she had wanted to believe that the internment stemmed from a judicial error that the authorities might soon set aright. As time passed, however, her attention shifted to the camp itself, which she contended served no purpose in a communist regime. If protestors and opponents were unhappy in North Korea, it was enough to simply kick them out. Running a camp such as Yodok was a crime, a concentration of inhumanity. Eventually, she went still further, asserting that though North Korea still wore the badge of communism, it had lost its soul. I think it was only then that she truly realized she'd been had.[11]

The prison uniform consisted of a purple jacket and trousers, which eventually became rags. Inmates were also given undershirts and briefs made of coarse linen and one pair of socks a year. In 10 years, Kang only received two uniforms. Within a short time, prisoners degenerated physically. "Their faces were ugly," Kang recalled in his book. "They had missing teeth, their hair was caked together and overgrown, and they were all filthy as animals. Yet more striking than their physical appearance was the aura of weakness that oozed from their every pore."[12] They seldom bathed and their clothes only got a natural wash when it rained.

Aside from the physical deprivation and hunger, the inmates' spirit was sapped by a pervasive mistrust engendered by the network of prisoners tasked with reporting on their fellows.

Kang and his sister went to prison school every morning and worked in the afternoon. Classes, which started at seven o'clock, were in Korean, math, biology, and politics. Portraits of Kim Il-sung and Kim Jong-il hung in the classroom. Beating and verbal abuse were routine. One teacher kicked and beat a little boy for complaining about having to do latrine duty and walked away when the boy fell into the septic pit. The boy climbed out but died a few days later. Schooling ended at age 15, when kids were considered adult and required to work all day. Prisoners worked in the fields and at a range of facilities in the camp complex, including a gypsum quarry and a gold mine, the toughest assignments. There were also farm produce plants and even a distillery producing snake liquor for export. The cushiest jobs were administrative.

In prison, Kang met Park Seung-jin, who had been a member of North Korea's 1966 World Cup soccer squad. (Kang claims the squad was imprisoned for having gone on a drinking binge in England, although North Korea has denied this charge and produced several surviving team members for the 2002 British TV documentary called "The Game of Their Lives."[13]) Park was still there 10 years later in 1987 when Kang and his family were released.

As far as he could figure, given the restrictions on movement, Kang believed that there were 10 "villages" in Yodok. Four were for criminals and minor offenders. The ordinariness of these minor offenses boggles the mind. Some were convicted for not turning up to political rallies. Six villages were for political prisoners who would never be released. This latter group included condemned spies, families of landowners and capitalists, and purged Party members. By the mid-1990s, Yodok may have been holding as many as 70,000 people. This was the estimate given by a former prisoner, identified by his surname Lee, who was interviewed by Human Rights Watch after his defection to South Korea.[14] From 1995 to 1998, Lee worked on a logging unit in the different sections of the camp, which allowed him to move around and get a sense of the overall scale of the facility. His crime was that his brother had been arrested for trying to sell uranium.

Families of North Korean defectors to South Korea are severely punished, which is why many conceal their names when they arrive in South Korea. The most prominent in Yodok was the family of Hwang Jang-yop, the architect of the *Juche* ideology, who defected to South Korea in 1997. Because of this tradition of punishing families for the crimes of individual members, South Koreans have always felt ambiguous about the individual defectors who come from the North, leaving family members behind to face punishment.

We may assume that the South Korean soldiers who snuck into North Korea on spying missions and who were caught would have been executed, but it is possible that citizens accused of helping them may be included among these lifers. Among those serving life sentences would also be people who opposed Kim Jong-il's succession. It is not known for sure if there have been any serious attempts to unseat Kim Jong-il. There have been reports of various incidents over the years, but there are no details. In the 1970s, the captain of a Japanese ship was handed a letter requesting help from the Tokyo government for a rebel group. In 1980, a government minister was quoted as saying that there were opponents to the succession.[15] There was reportedly once an attempt to blow up the Kim Il-sung Immortality Tower in the city of Wonsan. A defector, Kang Myong-do, the son of a prime minister, claimed that some elite officers had planned to kill the leadership on the rostrum during a military parade in April 1992, and stage a coup. This group of 40 officers was allegedly led by the Deputy Chief of Staff, Ahn Jong-ho.[16] Whether this plot was real or was tortured out of people, we may assume that those associated with it, and any other such incidents, who were not executed would be among the lifers in camps such as Yodok.

For these villagers, there is no need to display portraits of the Great and Dear Leaders, no self-criticism sessions, no attempt at re-education. It is believed they are used to construct highly sensitive military facilities, whose secrets die with them. Their heads are shaved to make them instantly recognizable if they escape.

According to Kang, anyone attempting to escape was publicly executed. When he reached adulthood, Kang was required to attend these events. He saw 15 in five years. When victims tried to scream their innocence, guards would stuff stones in their mouths. Usually, victims were tied to a post and shot. But once, two former soldiers who had evaded recapture for several days were hung. One died quickly, but the other wriggled in agony on the end of the rope for some time. When he was dead, the thousands of prisoners present were required to throw stones at the corpses. The shredded remains were left dangling overnight.

The Yodok prisoners lived on a diet of corn, 500 grams a day for a working adult and 400 grams for a child, supplemented by some homegrown vegetables and herbs picked on the mountain slopes. Kang later learned how to trap rats, which provided valuable protein. The worst season, surprisingly, was spring. After struggling through the bitter Korean winter, bodies relaxed and many fell sick and died. Some also killed themselves, although this form of escape brought more punishment upon surviving family members in the form of extended sentences or transfer to a harsher camp. Kang's father and uncle came close to suicide on one occasion. Kang wrote:

> When I got home from work my grandmother told me the two of them had gone up to the mountains with the intention of hanging themselves from a tree. I started to shake uncontrollably, then threw myself on my mat and

thought about them as hard as I could, muttering, 'Come back, come back.' I don't know how long I had been this way when I heard the shack door creak open. It was them! I cried from happiness."[17]

Kim Yong was a prisoner in the Kechon camp.[18] He grew up in an orphanage. In North Korea, orphans are unusually lucky in one respect, in that blood lineage does not create doubts abut their loyalty. He was initially told his father had been killed by a bomb in the Korean War. Kim Yong became a Party member and a State Security Bureau official. His life changed in 1993 when it came out that his father had actually been accused of being a CIA spy and executed in 1957. Although he never knew his father, when this connection was revealed, Kim was sent to Kechon prison, where he was put to work in a mine. His fellow prisoners included individuals and families of individuals charged with rebellion, criticizing Kim Jong-il, spying, and even pacifism. In 1996, Kim was transferred to a facility called the 18th Administrative Camp, which housed both political offenders and ordinary criminals in separate sections.[19] There, incredibly, he discovered his mother. She had been in the camp since 1957, put away when her husband was executed. Kim escaped in 1998 and now lives in South Korea.

Ahn Myong-chol was a guard at four prisons before defecting to South Korea. He was 19 when he started work at Hoeryong Prison. Ahn was told that he could kill any prisoner who tried to escape or attack him.[20] In fact, guards who killed a would-be escapee earned the right to go to college, which led to the murder of some innocent prisoners.

Ahn tells the tragic story of a woman who had been in Hoeryong since she was five years old after her uncle was purged and his entire family put away. This lady's mother and brother had died of starvation. When she was 26, a guard raped her. As sexual relations were banned in the camp, the officer had his rank reduced and the woman was sent to a punishment center. The next time Ahn saw her, the woman's body had burns all over it. Some time later, he saw her dragging herself around the camp on a rubber tire. A coal wagon had run over her legs, which had been amputated below the knee.

Her name was Han Jin-duk.

10

The One Fat Man

In the finance and accounting department of the ruling Workers' Party, there is an office dedicated to the management of Kim Jong-il's health. The worthies in the "Longevity Institute," as it's called, are tasked with making sure that he gets the best food.[1]

For example, his rice comes from special farms in Mundok County, north of the capital, where each grain is individually examined. In a book written after his defection to South Korea, Kim Jong-il's nephew, Lee Han-yong, revealed that the rice has to be cooked over a flame, using firewood from Mt. Paekdu. The bottled mineral water he drinks is the regular North Korean "Sindok" brand, but comes from a dedicated spring.

Early on, Kim Jong-il realized that there was a whole world of taste out there beyond his country's borders. In 1977, he reportedly had his overseas embassies gather samples of foreign cigarette brands. After personal research, he narrowed his preference down to Rothmans and Dunhill. He finally opted for Rothmans. Rather than import, in revolutionary *Juche* fashion, he arranged for the production of a similar-tasting local brand called "Paektusan," the North's English spelling at the time for Mt. Paekdu (*san* means "mountain" in Korean). But not all quality items can be reproduced so easily. Some years ago a representative for Hennessy confirmed for me that Kim Jong-il was the company's biggest single customer for its Paradis cognac. Kim was apparently spending around US$700,000 a year on it. (Interestingly, my informant explained, Paradis purchasing patterns offer an indicator of political stability. Higher sales usually mean an increase in gift-giving by the leader to key people to keep them sweet. In other words, an increase in sales equals a rise in political nervousness.)

In recent years, Kim has made efforts to improve his health. He tried to quit smoking in 1982 and finally managed to do it in 1999. Typically, all the top military commanders followed suit. He was a heavy drinker until he was 50, when his doctors finally persuaded him to drop the hard liquor.[2] He now drinks half a bottle of red wine a day. His preferences are Bordeaux and Burgundy; for the Russia trip in 2001, he had a consignment delivered to the train from Paris.

The pampering is perhaps to be expected of an East Asian dictator. Food has long been an obsession for Koreans — "have you eaten rice today?" used to be the common greeting in the South — and they are among the world's big consumers of exotic parts of exotic animals. We should not be surprised, then, that Kim Jong-il is something of a foodie fusspot.

He's not the kind of leader who would slurp a bowl of noodles with the workers, but then nor is he the type to slip an apron on and start flipping his own pancakes. He defers to outside experts, and, having got over his kidnapping phase, he prefers to hire them. A few years ago, North Korean officials hired two Italian chefs to make pizzas for Kim Jong-il and teach the locals how to do it. Their story highlights Kim Jong-il's luxurious lifestyle.

> Presently we came to an enormous gate at the end of an avenue with a guard inside a building. A green light flashed on the hood of the car and the gate rose. The

guard made a kind of queer waving gesture at us as we passed and suddenly we found ourselves inside a magnificent park with trees and flower beds and fountains and manicured lawns surrounding a strange building made up of two square shaped wings, each about 150 meters long. One of the wings was four floors high, the other was lower and had no windows at all; the two wings were connected by [a] narrow lower structure. There were no signs in this hotel, no reception counter, no room keys.[3]

This was one of Kim's palaces. Life wasn't all peacocks and croquet, though. On one occasion, Kim Jong-il or some of his guests, dining on a pleasure boat, complained about the food prepared by his Italian chefs.

That evening we had a light dinner back at the base: a pair of lobsters, salad and French white wine. The phone rang. Mr Om put down his glass of Remy Martin which we had been downing by the bucketful and went to answer. It was always a stressful moment for him: his daily progress report and communicating the preparations for the next day. Suddenly the expression on Mr Om's face darkened visibly as he listened in silence to who I think must have been Mr Pak on the other end complaining that the food had not met with approval.

After our wives had been sent scuttling to bed, the Chef and I were led into an office and subjected to a classic brainwashing session. Actually, the problem hadn't been the pizza at all, but the lamb. It had been allowed to marinate for two days. This was followed by the immense labor of preparing the garnish with little bundles of dried spaghetti which I had tasted myself. It was really an exquisite dish, visually stunning, but, alas, somebody had found it too salty. So that night until one o'clock we were obliged to stay up and revise the entire program, with Mr Om removing anything that was deemed too salty.[4]

Konstantin Pulikovskiy's account of Kim Jong-il's 2001 cross-Russia train ride also provides some insight into this fussiness. Kim Jong-il brought along North Korean chefs trained in France who were able to rustle up Korean, Russian, Chinese, Japanese, and French dishes. Kim and Pulikovskiy discussed the menu every day. Lobsters and other fresh food were flown in at four points on the journey. *Kimchi*, the spicy Korean side dish, was a staple. Kim explained to his host that the strong seasoning in *kimchi* provided a necessary substitute for an enzyme needed for digestion which only the Koreans, among *homo sapiens*, lack. (Such myths are commonplace among Koreans. Another is that Koreans were relatively unaffected by the SARS virus that swept through East Asia in 2003 because they were protected by *kimchi*.)

Kim Jong-il may be a bit of a germophobe. In Khabarovsk in 2001, he was taken to a milk processing plant, where he was invited to taste the cottage cheese and vitamin-enriched milk. He declined, which was a little rude.

However, it would be a mistake to assume that Kim Jong-il is a pig. He's a gourmet, not a glutton. He enjoys the flavors and textures of food, and eats in modest portions. In St. Petersburg, the local governor, alerted by Pulikovskiy to Kim's preferences, served up salted pork fat, *pelmen* (dumplings) and pickled cucumbers — an appetizer which he clearly enjoyed, for he recalled it several times afterwards.

"Chairman Kim's table was filled with expensive dishes from around the world," Kim Jong-il's former Japanese chef, Kenji Fujimoto, told the Japanese daily *Sankei Shimbun*. "He enjoyed rich *sushi* such as *toro*, made with delicate tuna-belly flesh, and *uni*, sea-urchin egg *sushi*."[5] He is apparently so partial to shark-fin soup that he'll have it up to three times a week. Fujimoto said that in mid-summer, Kim Jong-il, following Korean tradition, likes to eat *boshintang*, dog soup. In his forties, he was instructed by East German doctors to lose weight. Over a couple of months in 1980, he ran up and down the steps in front of his house, with his son and nephew in tow, and lost 20 kilos. But he soon put it back on.[6]

Modest portions notwithstanding, Kim Jong-il remains a chubby fellow. To be more precise, in North Korea he is *the* chubby fellow. He's the only Fat Bastard in the whole country. What makes his lifestyle so revolting is that, while he's been sticking his beak into glasses of Burgundy and moaning about the lamb, 10 percent of his country's population has died of famine.

Less than 20 percent of the country is suitable for arable farming, but North Koreans managed. Until the 1980s, North Korea was self-sufficient in food, but then, to feed the growing population, the country started to import a small amount of grain, mostly from China. The government undertook some projects to expand farmland. But land reclamation off the west coast didn't work well. Clearance of mountain slopes for terrace farming proved disastrous. Planners failed to anticipate the need to build up effective banks and the first rains washed off the topsoil, which then ran into streams and silted up rivers. By the 1990s, the Soviet barter trade and low "friendship prices" had dried up due to the collapse of European Communism, and the Chinese were demanding payment in dollars. Around the time, Kim Jong-il was being advised to go easy on the hard liquor, North Korean citizens were being encouraged to tighten their belts and have just two meals a day. Then, in a move to contain the serious and growing food shortage, government food distribution to the mountainous northeast region was stopped altogether. To maintain the fiction that it provided for all its citizens' material needs, the communist government denied it was in trouble. "What's wrong with importing food?" an economics minister snapped back at me during a 1992 interview when I asked if the country was doing so.

Bad weather in 1995 turned a serious problem into a crisis. In September 1995, the regime made an international appeal for help, claiming that the heavy summer rains had ruined the harvest. This admission was very unusual and offered an early clue to the extent of the country's troubles. North Korea had held its begging bowl out in front of its communist allies in the past, but it had never asked for charity from its enemies. A United Nations study that year revealed that the country could meet only around 50 percent of its food requirements. However, such was the collective mistrust of North Korea that this shocking statistic failed to galvanize the international community. North Korea would now reap the harvest of lies and belligerent nastiness it had sown for so long.

International aid bodies set up in Pyongyang, but North Korean government officials mindlessly denied them access to information. On his first visit, Andrew Natsios of World Vision US, a non-governmental organization (NGO), found that officials were lying about conditions to the very people who wanted to help. In his book, *The Great North Korean Famine*, he wrote:

> The expatriate NGO and UN staff members whom I met at the airport displayed a level of cynicism, anger, and frustration I have never seen in any other emergency anywhere in the world. Many argued that there was no emergency, that no one was dying, and that the international community should not be there. They said they were tired of the daily diet of manipulation, deceit, and propaganda fed to them by the authorities. I left the country only a week later feeling much the same.[7]

Before foreign aid workers entered an area, wrote Natsios, dead bodies, beggars, and emaciated children were removed from the streets, and only Party members were allowed out of their homes to receive food aid.[8]

Despite the spectacle of its utter failure, the regime never for a moment faltered in its willingness to sacrifice and suppress the citizenry in the interests of its own political survival. The regime's unrelenting arrogance was demonstrated in its attitude to donors. Authorities told citizens that the real intention of aid workers was to undermine the communist system. In 1995, Japan shipped 450,000 tons of grain. The North Korean authorities told the citizens that Japan was trying to atone for its colonial rule. In that same year, South Korea sent 150,000 tons. Kim Jong-il was admired for getting his enemies to refill the grain silos. To show what a tough guy he was, around the same time he authorized spying missions against South Korea. In 1996, a North Korean spy submarine ran aground off the South Korean coast. Because of this, and because of stories that the aid was going to the army, in 1996 and 1997 Seoul started lobbying foreign countries not to send aid.

As the ration system broke down, people foraged for edible weeds and roots, authorities lifted internal travel restrictions to allow people to visit relatives in parts of the country where food distribution was better, and military units raided collective farm stocks. Women tried not to get pregnant. Some families abandoned their elderly. In other cases, the elderly gave their rations to younger family members. Some parents abandoned their children. Others gave their food to their children and starved themselves. The elite had access to food, as did, interestingly, the farmers. But in the large towns and cities, there was desperation. People were dying in droves. The good and the meek went first. The mean, the resourceful, and the lucky found ways to survive. Children joined gangs foraging for food, and teachers bullied students to bring them food. Thievery became widespread. There were even reports of cannibalism.

By the spring of 1998, the worst was over. A new government in South Korea, under veteran dissident Kim Dae-jung, introduced a policy of engagement with the North and sent generous shipments of fertilizer. This, along with US, Chinese, Japanese, and EU food aid helped to stop the famine. Exact figures are not known, but South Korean intelligence has referred to a population survey by the North Korean authorities in the summer of 1998 which put the death toll at somewhere just under three million.[9] It is not known if this survey counted the gulag population. It's also possible that hundreds of thousands who fled to China are counted by officials in their hometowns as "disappeared, presumed dead."

But this is fine-tuning. For a country with a population of only 23 million and situated in one of the most economically vibrant regions of the globe, the figures are staggeringly inexcusable. For the cause of the catastrophe, we need look no further than the incompetence of the regime headed by the one fat man in the country. Instead of adjusting the agriculture and distribution systems to meet the challenge of food shortages, Kim Jong-il and his fellow party animals continued to commit resources to defense and internal policing.

Conditions continue to be extremely harsh. Even in 2003, five years after the end of the famine, international aid continues to take care of an estimated one third of the population. The health service is in tatters. "Life for the average North Korean is a grim struggle for survival, but the resilience and dignity of the people is impressive," said Kathi Zellweger of the Catholic charity Caritas.[10]

A United Nations–European Union survey in 2002 classified 10 percent of North Korean children as "acutely malnourished" and 40 percent as "chronically malnourished." An average seven-year-old boy in North Korea is now 20 centimeters shorter and 10 kilos lighter than his brother in South Korea. They are the stunted generation.[11]

Hundreds of thousands of ordinary North Koreans continue to risk arrest and even execution to cross into China in search of food and hope. There they live with relatives, or make homes in holes in the woods, hiding from Chinese police. South Korean and international activists estimate that 300,000 North Koreans have melted into the three bordering Chinese provinces, where there was already a large ethnic Korean population. Tens of thousands of women have been trafficked to brothels and farmed out as wives for Chinese farmers. A daughter fetches $25.[12]

Amazingly, the ragged state remains fanatically obsessed with anything that opposes its claims to be a "workers' paradise." China conspires. Beijing's agreement with Pyongyang to return refugees takes precedence over Beijing's obligations under the United Nations Refugee Convention. Korean migrants caught by Chinese police and sent back across the border face prison. For serious offenses — such as repeated crossings; contact with South Koreans, foreign missionaries, aid workers, or journalists; going to a church; having sex with foreigners; or trying to apply for political asylum — a refugee faces a life sentence or even execution.

Many North Koreans going back and forth across the border are smugglers. In a bid to maintain control, authorities have periodically cracked down on smuggling. In one typical case, in 1999, four women were publicly executed for trying to smuggle goods into China. They got the death penalty because the goods in question weighed over five kilos. Some 500 people gathered at the farmers' market for the execution. It was mid-summer, but the victims, their heads shaved, were dressed in winter clothes to prevent blood from spilling over the ground. They were shot, with family members present, by four men.

There is no movement southward toward the heavily fortified DMZ, because the chances of capture are so much higher, because there is no possibility concealing the motive to defect, and also because, for most North Koreans, the South remains the enemy. It's not until they reach China that they are able to unlearn the anti-South propaganda they have grown up with. Meanwhile, the trickle of refugees making it through China to South Korea has increased to a steady stream. Until the 1990s, one or two a year escaped. In 2002, the pace rose to 1,200. At the time of writing, the United States was considering allowing the immigration of North Korean refugees.

The increasing flow of refugees and defectors is indicative of a larger development within North Korea. That is, the deliberate starving of the eastern provinces, the nationwide famine, and the failure of the regime to provide basic rations and material support have combined to end the myth of the "workers' paradise" and the benevolent leadership of Kim Jong-il. Aid workers in China report that North Koreans coming over the border in 2003 are much more critical of Kim Jong-il and his regime than they were even during the famine. In early 1998, security officials reportedly uncovered a planned mutiny by army officers in Hamhung, the east coast industrial city at the epicenter of the famine. Kim Jong-il may still have North Koreans in his control, but he is no longer in their hearts.

In her evocative documentary about North Korean refugees in China, "Shadows and Whispers," Korean-American film-maker Kim Jung-eun asked some young boys to sing a song they had been taught about the fatherly leader Kim Jong-il. They sang hesitatingly.

When they had finished, one boy paused thoughtfully and mumbled, "Some father."

CHAPTER

11

Submerging Market

There will be no solution to North Korea's chronic food problems until Kim Jong-il's regime changes its economic system (or is itself changed). Even when this happens, the country will still require development aid for many years. North Korea is, to mangle the jargon of the stock market analyst, a submerged market emerging from a worse-than-expected decade, going toward nowhere.

It's hard to know precisely how bad the economy is because Pyongyang stopped publishing meaningful statistics in the mid-1960s (when the rival South started growing), and started releasing the "Thanks to the Great Leader, mining has increased by 10 percent this year" — over what, who knows? — type of annual report. In Seoul, the Bank of Korea makes the best stab at compiling statistics of the North. It says that the northern economy has shriveled by around 40 percent since 1990. Such figures are derived from what's available, such as an admission by Pyongyang that its budget revenues, which represent some 89–90 percent of national income, declined by almost half between 1992 and 1996.

As we have seen, the rot began with the collapse of the Soviet Union, its longtime benefactor, in 1989. Under the Soviets' "friendship" pricing, the North had been importing oil and other raw materials for up to a quarter of the going international rate. But in the 1990s North Korea had to pay real prices with real money, which it didn't have much of because it wasn't selling much overseas and wasn't in good enough standing with foreign banks to borrow.

In 1999, the North Korean economy stopped shrinking. Growth was recorded at 6.2 percent, the first positive figure in nine years.[1] The historic inter-Korean summit of 2000, which won South Korea's Kim Dae-jung the Nobel Peace Prize, led to an expansion of economic activity with the South. North Korean diplomatic relations have since revived with Australia and have been established with Canada and all EU states, save Ireland and France, and links with Russia and China have been improved. These developments led to growth of 1.3 percent in 2000 and 3.7 percent in 2001. Gross national income in 2001 was US$15.7 billion, representing per capita income of US$706.

Structurally, the economy is similar to that of South Korea in the late 1960s when it was beginning to industrialize: around one-third services, one-third agriculture (farming, forestry, and fisheries), and one-third industry (manufacturing, mining, and construction). By 2001, trade was US$2.27 billion, an increase of 15.1 percent, but still way below the 1990 level when it was US$4.2 billion. The growth is evenly spread between imports and exports. Notably, 2001 saw a big rise in overseas shipments of primary products such as fish, shellfish, and base metals, a result of imported equipment for livestock and fish farms, and extraction equipment for mines. Japan was North Korea's biggest market in 2001, buying almost as much as its other top 10 trading partners combined. China was the main source of imports and biggest partner overall. A factor here is China's role as a middleman for North–South Korea trade, for South Korea is now a significant partner. In the first nine months of 2002, inter-Korea trade was US$343.07 million, up 17.9 percent on 2001. Overall, foreign trade is still two-thirds imports, with the deficit financed partly by missile sales and possibly some aid from China.

But let's not get too excited. According to one 2001 study, North Korea needs a minimum outside investment of US$1 billion a year for five years — and, we should add, needs to use it wisely — to stop the economic shriveling and escape the "poverty trap." Actual reconstruction would take a lot more capital. Where would this kind of money come from? Most banks shudder at the mere mention of North Korea, which is notorious for refusing to pay debts.

Estimates of the country's outstanding debt vary, but it is believed to be over US$12 billion. Several billion is owed to Moscow, which we may assume is philosophical about ever getting it back. Similarly, Pyongyang may interpret its agreement to repay the US$4.6 billion financed by the Korea Energy Development Organization (KEDO) for the two light-water reactors in a couple of decades as a "face" measure, and may not be thinking of repaying. That brings us down to around a US$3 billion outstanding principal plus interest owed to western banks. Some of these debts go back to Pyongyang's first skirmish with western banks in the early 1970s, when the leadership ordered a few hundred Volvos for its top officials and never paid up.

Treatment of investors is equally shabby. The most successful are there for political reasons — some Japanese-Koreans with family ties have set up a range of joint ventures. There is some Taiwanese computer business, some Thai textile operations, and a handful of joint venture restaurants, but not much else. In the 1990s, a Belgian businessman with a diamond-cutting operation provided the best foreign business success story in Pyongyang. He would bring in diamonds from South Africa, cut them in North Korea, and dispatch them to Europe for sale. One of his breakthroughs was to discover a way around the government's refusal to allow him to pay incentive bonuses to his North Korean workers. He hit upon the idea of bringing in consumer goods to distribute to top performers, and in two months, production doubled. But even he eventually went the way of all non-Korean flesh, somehow upsetting the authorities and being closed down.

All in all, there's not a lot of positive experience to convince foreigners of the joys of investing in the "workers' paradise." The obvious answer is for the big South Korean conglomerates like Hyundai, Samsung and LG that built up the South to step in and undertake projects in the North, and for banks to lend to them under South Korean government guarantees. But even these companies may not have the stomach for it. During South Korea's nation-building period — the 1960s, 1970s and 1980s — these companies did not have to worry much about profit, paying workers well, or repaying loans. Now they are required to be profitable and may find that North Korea is not worth the risk. Perhaps, North Korea will need to found its own Hyundais and Samsungs and hire South Koreans as executives and consultants.

But, we are getting ahead of ourselves.

What everyone is waiting for in the early 2000s is a sign that North Korea is turning the corner and heading in the direction of market reforms, following the Chinese and Vietnamese model. In July 2002, it appeared as if something along these lines were happening. Pyongyang abolished its rationing system and introduced new "market" prices in the public service sector. At the same time wages for Party and government officials, company employees, and the military were raised. It is even believed that a special ration system enjoyed by the elite Party officials for eggs and other special food was abolished.

This was exciting stuff, for outside observers at least.

For North Koreans, it was a little startling. Under the new pricing, a kilo of subsidized rice on the ration system went up from 0.13 North Korean won (NKW) to NKW44. The streetcar fare went up tenfold to NKW1.[2] Salary increases were not quite commensurate with the price changes. While goods rose at least 25-fold, average monthly wages increased only 20-fold to around

NKW2,000. To put this in perspective, workers now had to spend around 50 percent of their wages on food, compared to the around 3.5 percent they spent under the old rationing system. While miners and other workers in tough or strategic industries got the 20–25-fold raise, "professionals" and those in "leadership and non-production areas" got 19-fold and 17-fold increases respectively. Farmers were reported to accept the changes because they translated into more side income for produce raised on allotments. But for others it was tough, especially given reports that many companies were unable to pay the salaries.

At the same time, the exchange rate was normalized. The US dollar, which for years could be changed into local currency for around NKW2, now costs NKW150. The idea of this was to pull in those dollars being exchanged on the black market for over NKW200. However, one effect has reportedly been to push the black market NKW/US$ rate up to over NKW700.

The reforms were reminiscent of changes in China in 1984, which went on to have a deep impact. However, the purpose of the North Korean reforms appears to have been to crack down on the black markets, to which so much economic activity had moved, and to get people back to work. In other words, what appeared to be "market reforms" represented an effort to normalize the production process under the old system, rather than to alter it.

This interpretation was supported in late September 2002, when the Party's *Rodong Shinmun* daily editorialized thus: "The capitalist culture could be defined largely as the law of the jungle, aversion to human nature, extreme hedonism and decadent lifestyle." North Korea's socialist society "will not tolerate such inhuman culture," the paper said. "The reckless exchange of culture with other nations poisons socialism and crushes our national dignity and unique culture."

It's possible that such propaganda was intended to keep the masses in check while the leadership took its first wobbly free market steps. Why else, we may ask, would Kim Jong-il's brother-in-law, Chang Song-taek, have led a high-level economic fact-finding visit to South Korea just after that editorial? Chang's delegation visited the POSCO iron and steel works at Pohang, Samsung Electronics, Hyundai Motors, Busan port, and other key industrial sites. And why, since around 2001, as aid workers and diplomats report, has North Korea increasingly been sending officials overseas to learn about international law, economy and trade?[3]

Whatever lies behind such steps, it has become painfully obvious that the only real hope for North Korea is market reform and that it needs South Korean help to do it. This is a tough reality because it turns the northern regime's whole reason for existence — the need to "liberate" the South — on its head.

Fortunately for Kim Jong-il, the South no longer dreams of the North's collapse. In fact, Seoul's engagement policy grew partly out of an aversion to the idea of having to absorb the North if it were to collapse. The cost would be so unbearably high, in both economic and social terms, that both the government and people of South Korea overwhelmingly opposed any form of rapid unification. What they'd rather do is to help the North grow under its own steam, which, for now, means propping up the regime of Kim Jong-il.

This process of helping North Korea grow has begun, but it is slow because of mistrust on the part of the North and its fear of becoming a South Korean colony if things go too fast. The areas likely to develop are: trade of North Korean seafood products and minerals; processing-on-commission trade with South Korea (for example, turning southern fabric into suits and shipping them back to the fabric supplier for sale in the South); and light manufacturing in special economic zones. Primary industries such as tourism are also likely cash earners.

We are already seeing movement in these areas. Several hundred small and medium South Korean companies take advantage of the cheaper labor and engage in the processing-on-commission trade, often through China. But it is the special economic zones that grab attention.

Pyongyang has been toying with special economic zones for foreign investment for some time, but can't get it right. The first attempt was an area of 300 square miles around the ports of Rajin and Sonbong in North Korea's remote northeast, where it converges with the borders of China and Russia. Now known as "Rason" since the merger of the two ports, the zone was part of a US$30 billion UN development program in the early 1990s, along with China's Yanbian Korean Autonomous Prefecture and Russia's Primorsky Territory. The attraction was the ice-free Korean ports, which could serve the frozen Russian Far East and the land-locked Manchurian hinterland. Clearly, some people in Pyongyang had big hopes. Rason was touted as a gateway to Europe, the "Rotterdam of the East."[4]

Among the investors in this zone is Dalmorproduct, Russia's mammoth seafood company, which has 52 ships based at Rason, providing catches for a state-run plant that exports to Japan and South Korea. The Emperor Group Hotel and Casino, owned by Hong Kong tycoon Albert Yeung, is a US$63 million complex on an otherwise empty coast catering to Chinese gamblers. It is the biggest FDI project in North Korea.[5] There is also a Soviet-built thermonuclear power station in this region which uses the 500 tons of crude oil which the US was shipping until November 2002 as part of the KEDO deal. It supplies around 10 percent of the country's power.

But these investments were not enough. Trade through Rason dropped from US$310 million in 1993 to one-tenth of that figure by 1998, when full-scale development was abandoned. Across the border, the Chinese zone in Yanbian didn't do too badly, attracting US$1.6 billion in mainly Chinese and South Korean investment in 10 years. Rason's hope for the future is that plans to link the Trans-Siberian Railway to South Korea materialize and lead to renewed investment.

The sheer remoteness of Rason sent the message to investors that they were not really wanted. Not so with the Keumgang Mountain project. The story of the plan to turn the beautiful mountain region in southeastern North Korea into a free zone, and the development so far, provide useful illustration of the "Korean way" in which such projects are moved along.

The idea first came up, in 1989, when Hyundai Group founder Chung Ju-yung, the first southern businessman to meet Kim Il-sung, suggested that the Great Leader allow South Korean tourists to visit the area. Mr Chung, who was born in North Korea, saw this tourist venture as a simple way for the North to earn foreign currency. But Kim Il-sung was suspicious of the capitalist Chung.

Two years later, the Reverend Sun-myung Moon, the founder of the Unification Church and also North Korea-born, visited his homeland and proposed turning the Keumgang region into a free zone for international tourism. Around this time, we should note, the cash being sent to Kim Il-sung by *Chosen Soren*, the pro-North Korea residents' association in Japan, was beginning to dry up. It is possible that the Great Leader saw Moon's Unification Movement as a potential new source of funding, for he gave the go-ahead. A feasibility study was conducted, a plan drawn up to include an array of tourism facilities and an industrial complex for light industry, and a full-scale model built. But three problems prevented the project from getting off the ground: the government in Seoul would not agree to let tourists go north, the northern military were not happy with the idea of visitors so near to its side of the DMZ, and the Unification Church fell into debt and its funds dried up. This last problem meant that by the time the first two were solved, with the election of President Kim Dae-jung in Seoul in 1997, Hyundai was able to step back in and take over a project it had always considered its own.

The Hyundai founder broke the ice with the North Koreans to restart the initiative by delivering 500 cows through the DMZ truce village of Panmunjom. In a gesture typical of the emotionalism that drives overseas Korean interest in the North and which works wonders with their communist brethren, this gift represented a homecoming for North Korea-born Chung, who had decades earlier stolen a cow from his father and left home to make his fortune.

In November 1998, the first boatload of southern tourists sailed up the east coast and docked in North Korea. It was a historic moment for the two countries. By the end of 2001, 400,000 South Koreans had made the trip. In addition, Hyundai had built crucial ties with the North's leery leadership on behalf of South Korea. But at some cost. In addition to having to pay for and build all facilities, Hyundai was obliged to pay US$12 million a month for a guaranteed minimum target number of tourists, which it was never able to meet. To save costs, the company pushed for a road to allow tourists to be bussed across the DMZ. In September 2002, the two governments agreed on this and on a rail link up the east cost. South Korea's official Korea National Tourist Organization became a partner to keep the project afloat. Despite heavy losses, Hyundai has soldiered on in the hope that the endeavor will win Kim Jong-il's trust and position it to make profits elsewhere.

The next zone to be announced was on the border with China. In September 2002, North Korea said that the city of Sinuiju would be made a Special Administrative Region. This news came with unusual fanfare. Reporters from *AP Dow Jones* and *The Asian Wall Street Journal* were invited to Pyongyang to cover the story. This was probably due to the influence of the man whom Pyongyang anointed as the zone's governor, Chinese-born Dutch orchid magnate Yang Bin.

You have to wonder why the most xenophobic regime in the galaxy would hand over the reins of a flagship project to a foreigner. Clearly, this was Kim Jong-il's personal choice and one that gives a sense of how North Korea is ruled by one, sometimes whimsical, man. There are three explanations: first, Kim Jong-il does not think his own people are up to it. He has said this much to South Korean businessmen in private conversations. Second, Yang showed good faith by making horticultural investments in the North. Third, aside from seeing opportunity, Yang may have caught the missionary bug that infects so many when confronted with North Koreans, and slapped down some very big bucks. This may be what upset the Chinese authorities, for they promptly detained Yang on charges of fraud, tax evasion, and bribery, adding to the sense of the bizarre. Clearly, China had not been consulted about Yang's appointment, which was odd, as Sinuiju was just across the Yalu River from the Chinese city of Dandong, where there were discussions with Seoul for an industrial complex exclusively for South Korean firms. (That agreement was signed in November 2002.)[6]

Like all North Korean cities except Pyongyang, Sinuiju is a scruffy, run-down place. If you're coming by train from Beijing, this is where, after the long ride through Manchuria, everything seems to go quiet. The engine is changed and a dining car added, featuring a sparse menu and the pictures of Kim Il-sung and Kim Jong-il on the wall. The city has machinery, metal, chemical fiber, and consumer goods industries, but looks sleepy compared to Dandong. The zone would include the entire city and a planned port 30 kilometers away at the mouth of the Yalu. South Korean companies are interested in infrastructure projects, but Chinese companies are expected to make up most of the investment. The vision is for it to become an international financial and commercial center. Seriously. Before his arrest, Yang had given some ideas as to how this might get started. Yang had planned that Sinuiju's current population of 200,000 would be moved out, and around half a million skilled workers be brought in. The city then was to have been walled off.[7] Yang also said that the city would be almost entirely demolished and rebuilt. A special law for the zone guarantees religious freedom, private property, the right to strike, freedom of the press, publication, association and protest, all of which seem distinctly non-North Korean. It's somehow hard to imagine Pyongyang not sticking its nose in, but the law says central government would only intervene in the event of "war or armed insurgency."

As North Korea's Sinuiju is to China, so Kaesong is to South Korea.[8] Just 78 kilometers from Seoul and a stone's throw from the Panmunjom truce village in the DMZ, Kaesong (population 400,000) was Korea's ancient dynastic capital before Seoul and was part of South Korea until the Korean War.

When Hyundai officials suggested an industrial park in either Kaesong or the nearby port of Haeju, Kim Jong-il repeatedly asked them instead to help develop Sinuiju. Kim Jong-il was doubtful of the port facilities at Haeju and also suspicious of the southerners' interest in the sensitive military area near the DMZ. This went on for two years. Hyundai dispatched engineers to conduct an extensive feasibility study of Sinuiju, but they concluded that it would not attract manufacturing companies from the South. The main problem was that the harbor would need costly development to handle the ships bringing in the necessary raw materials to operate an industrial park. After reading Hyundai's study on Sinuiju in August 2000, Kim Jong-il accepted the plan for the South Korean firm to develop Kaesong instead.

"This area was South Korean before the war, and now I'm returning it to you without war," Kim told Hyundai officials. Two years later — there were other inter-Korea hiccups — the two governments agreed on the Kaesong project and started mine-clearing in the DMZ to reopen road and rail links.

The attraction of Kaesong is obvious. For many South Korean businesses, struggling under labor and logistics costs, the idea that a solution could be just an hour's drive from Seoul, and where the workers speak the same language and understand the orders you're barking at them, is heaven-sent. Kaesong forms a neat triangle with Seoul and the South Korean port of Incheon, the area in which almost half of the South's population is located. Hyundai polled Korean firms in China and found substantial interest in relocating to Kaesong were it to become available.

The plan calls for an industrial complex and a new town, to be developed in two phases by 2010. When completed, the zone would have 2,000 resident businesses employing 360,000 southerners and 250,000 northerners (a number promised by Kim Jong-il). They would produce US$15 billion annually. The area's ancient tombs and other historic buildings are forecast to attract over a million tourists a year.

Under a special law passed in November 2002, the zone is to be tariff- and visa-free, investments protected, and there will be no controls on foreign exchange transactions. Among other features, the basic monthly laboring wage will be set at under US$100, the Seoul Korean government said. This favorably compares with US$150 in China's Shenzen zone and suggests that Pyongyang has swallowed its pride about having "cheap labor." (In Rason, in the early 1990s, authorities took the suggestion that they set wages below the Chinese standard as an insult. Another example: Pyongyang was demanding US$700 a month for construction workers at the KEDO-run nuclear power site.) In contrast to the Sinuiju concept, Pyongyang would retain sovereignty and support a Kaesong Administrative Agency consisting of southerners and northerners who would issue the permits and run the zone. As the developer, Hyundai gets to recommend the head of the agency.

What to make of all this? In contrast to China, whose investment in infrastructure has given confidence to foreign investors, the most North Korea is doing is providing land. South Korea is paying for the infrastructure. For now, that is the extent of change in North Korea. Until there's more change, it's difficult to imagine any of these projects really taking off.

12

Follow The Money

Despite the economic shambles around him, Kim Jong-il has always had a sufficient supply of cash, to support his families and of course to use for political funds. Regardless of the ups and downs of the national economy, he has always been able to act the part of the generous dispenser. He once surprised Mikhail Kapitsa, a former Soviet deputy foreign minister who had been hunting with him, by sending over a truckload of pheasant and other game as a gift.[1] On another occasion, he wired his brother-in-law, Chang Song-taek, a million dollars. Chang had called from Macao, where he was on a trip with friends, to report that he'd lost all his money.[2]

At first jerk of the knee, such behavior strikes us as appalling. A million dollars would save a lot of lives in North Korea. In another sense, it shows a certain generosity. But to the South Korean observer, it very clearly shows Kim Jong-il's political skills. His are the actions of a traditional Korean boss. Those who rise to power in politics or business or organized crime must be able to secure funds and distribute them in a way that fulfils obligations to subordinates and supporters and that opens up new channels of influence. Hence the East Asian culture of strategic gift-giving which lies at the root of the region's endemic corruption. (In South Korea, politicians such as Kim Dae-jung and Kim Young-sam, both of whom later became presidents, survived as opposition factional bosses in an authoritarian political environment thanks largely to their ability to raise and skillfully distribute donations.)

In hungry North Korea, we expect that, as the leader, Kim Jong-il should be given the largest bowl in the soup kitchen. But you would expect some gestures — if not public appearances to console the suffering people, at least some kind of austerity. But there is no suggestion that he even skipped the occasional breakfast out of comradeship. He was immune from the suffering. While even his most earnest followers starved — some 50,000 Party members died in 1995 alone — he didn't even have to replace the fine wine with local plonk.[3] His conscience was clear because he was not taking from the nation's coffers. He has his own money supply.

So, where does it come from? This is a very pertinent question, because if we can identify the arteries through which the funds flow to the heart of the dictatorship, we can guess how the United States and South Korea and their allies might exercise the option of surgically tying them off.

The answer is that Kim Jong-il has his own conglomerate. Yes. He's a capitalist pig. His evil enterprise goes by the name of Division 39. Its operations are quite secretive and we may assume that only one or two people know their full extent. The irony is that this outcrop of capitalism is a special unit that lies quietly within the ruling Workers' Party, the very body that remains so committed to the idea of a socialist "workers' paradise" in North Korea.

Division 39 is reckoned to have generated as much as US$5 billion, which is kept safe in banks and operations in Switzerland, Macao, and elsewhere.[4] This staggering amount testifies to its importance. Division 39 is Kim Jong-il's Achilles heel.

Apparently set up in the mid-1970s to bankroll Kim Jong-il's political ambitions, Division 39's business activities are said to be organized into two broad categories. One is fronted by the Daesong Group, which owns the Daesong Bank and the Vienna-based Golden Star Bank. It also has other legitimate businesses. For example, Daesong is North Korea's biggest exporter of pine mushrooms and ginseng. It is involved in the seafood trade and mines gold, silver, and magnesium. Rather than seeking to increase production, the group decides how much it wants to make each year from, say, gold and then digs out the appropriate amount from the mines it controls for sale on the London bullion market. (Some mines are believed to be part of the so-called "Second Economy" controlled by the military.[5]) Many officials working for Daesong have studied abroad and have learned the ways of capitalist banking and trading systems.[6]

The other category of Division 39's business involves arms dealing and illegal projects, such as drug smuggling and counterfeiting of US dollars. Investigators in South Korea and Macao told *The Wall Street Journal* they reckoned that the trafficking of heroin and methamphetamines earns Kim Jong-il US$500 million a year. The street value of the North's methamphetamines in Japan, according to *Time*, may be as high as US$3 billion. The magazine quoted a recovering addict as saying that the North Korean product had been available for "at least twenty years." Some North Korean drugs are reportedly trafficked in South Korea. Others go to Russia, China, and Taiwan.

Somewhere between 4,200 and 7,000 hectares of farmland is for poppy growing.[7] North Koreans also hook up with international drug rings. Over the years, North Korean diplomats have been arrested with drugs, which may in fact be a method of fundraising embassies' budgets — meaning that not all goes to Division 39. Since 1977, over 20 North Korean diplomats have been nabbed in Russia, Egypt, Germany, China, Venezuela, India, Sweden, Zambia, Ethiopia, Laos, and Nepal. In a high-profile seizure in April 2003, Australian special forces intercepted a

North Korean vessel called *Pong Su* at sea and arrested 30 North Koreans on board on charges of smuggling 125 kilograms of heroin.

Kim Jong-il clearly knows that this is a naughty thing to do. "I have ordered that both drug dealers and drug users be shot," he told a Russian official when he was touring Russia in 2001. "As for the Chinese who promote the spread of illicit drugs, I have ordered that they be caned. If you come across any Korean drug addicts you have my permission to shoot them."[8]

It is highly likely that the US$450 million which Hyundai secretly sent to North Korea prior to the inter-Korean summit in 2000 went to Division 39. (In 2003, the incoming administration of President Roh Moo-hyun ordered an official inquiry into the illegal remittance, which was ostensibly to buy business licenses in connection with the Kaesong development zone and other projects, but which critics and even supporters of the engagement policy assume was a bribe. The top Hyundai executive at the center of the probe, Chung Mong-hun, son of the late founder, Chung Ju-yung, committed suicide in August 2003.)

Counterfeiting is another line of business. In 1994, several officials from a Daesong trading affiliate were arrested in Macao with US$250,000 in fake bills. This appears to have been part of a Division 39 project that slipped US$50 million in counterfeit dollars into the international banking system. The North Koreans, who are said to be very technically skilled, have reportedly expanded into production of Japanese yen and euros.

As outrageous as Division 39's international operations are, its free use of North Korean labor is pretty disgusting as well. North Korea places quotas on its people to furnish cash and product to Division 39. Citizens, for example, are required to gather mushrooms, clams, aralia shoots, and wild ginger roots, which Division 39 sells, according to defectors interviewed by *Time*.[9] Prisoners collect wild mushrooms, the elderly raise silkworms, and citizens sieve for particles of gold in rivers. All this gets sent to Division 39's Department No. 5.

"We never asked questions," a defector named Kim Yong-chul told *Time*. As a driver in a military unit, he delivered refined heroin to the dockside in the northeast port of Chongjin. "We thought we were showing our loyalty to Kim Jong-il. We thought he would use the money to improve our lives."[10]

Actually, Kim used it to improve his own.

13

Collision Course

There are in the world, it hardly need be said, a number of unpleasant states ruled by rather unpleasant people. North Korea is one.

Having said that, grasping the unpleasantness is not always easy, for it tends to hide. It does not threaten the visitor. This became apparent to me on my first trip to North Korea in 1989. Waiting in Beijing for three days for a tourist visa, I felt sick with apprehension, wondering if the North Koreans would see through the fiction that my three fellow travelers and I had created, and arrest us as spies. We were claiming to be innocent tourists working for the same company in Hong Kong. Actually, we were reporters who lived in South Korea. We had been careful to make sure we had no incriminating evidence, such as business cards or clothes with South Korean labels. Then, on the train through Manchuria, I discovered I was still carrying my Seoul Foreign Correspondents Club card and, worse, my pass to the US 8th Army base in Yongsan, Seoul. I cut them into small pieces and dropped them down the train's toilet, convinced all the time that I was being secretly watched.

Once in North Korea, though, I instantly relaxed. As foreigners, we felt very safe. The worst that could happen now was that we would be expelled.

Since then, I have to confess that I've always enjoyed my trips to North Korea. It is fascinating in a way that will be impossible for future generations to appreciate. It's Hitler's Germany and Stalin's Russia in the middle of Mao's Cultural Revolutionary madness. Visitors, of course, can view it from a safe place. That is not to say that there are not scary moments. Once, two of my colleagues were surrounded by a shouting mob after they took photographs at the Pyongyang Railroad Station and took the bold step of punching their way through and fleeing back to the hotel. Once I was indirectly threatened by an army general who asked me why I thought American troops were in South Korea. I told him I believed it was to defend against a possible North Korean invasion. "You have only half the truth," he said. "And people who have only half the truth can lose their life."

Another time our host at a boozy dinner, Workers' Party Secretary Kim Yong-soon, said his people were wondering if I was a South Korean spy. What got them going was a question I had asked a senior official about when they planned to remove the clause in the Party constitution that called for the communization of the South by whatever means. (The irony was that a South Korean diplomat in Beijing, who was one of my favorite North Korea analysts, had suggested this question to me.) Anyway, already slightly drunk, I started to wax philosophical about the nature of journalism as being rather like spying, except that everyone gets to see your reports, until my neighbor kicked me under the table.

There are also profound moments. Once, in the Myohyang Mountains, I took an early morning walk up a hill before the guides were awake. At one point, I could see a small military camp in the distance where soldiers were doing morning exercises. Walking up a wooded slope, I had the sensation that I was not alone. Over several steps, the impression formed, although I could not see anyone, that I was being accompanied by a large number of people wearing the traditional white garb of old Korea and that they were Korean War dead. This left me in an untypically emotional frame of mind.

There are also, of course, many amusing moments in North Korea. Damon Darlin of *The Wall Street Journal* was discovered rummaging on top of the garbage dump behind an apartment block in Pyongyang. He thought that by seeing what ordinary North Koreans threw out, he'd get a better glimpse of their lives. Interestingly, he found very little paper. Mostly cabbage leaves.

The truth is that in most cases, for foreigners, the unpleasantness of North Korea is deduced rather than directly experienced. But there is one way in which it manifests itself that binds foreigners in their dislike of the place. That is in that they are inevitably treated, albeit by otherwise polite and cheerful hosts, like the enemy. Visitors are cocooned, kept at a distance, chaperoned, and lied to. This is essentially why no foreigner likes North Korea. You can meet foreign consultants who talk positively about investment opportunities, aid workers who say that officials are doing their best, and experts who think that Kim Jong-il will come up with reforms. But scratch the surface and they all admit the place is vile.

This is quite a remarkable consensus.

We can, without fear of too much dispute, state North Korea's problem quite simply. Most other Asian nations have given up on dictatorship and, in varying degrees, have opted for economic growth and democratization. North Korea hasn't — simply because it has the wrong leadership.

It is its leadership that is the loser in the historic rivalry with the South. As a state, North Korea may survive for some time because South Koreans want to avoid absorbing it. But for the regime, it's just a matter of time before it either reforms or faces removal through internal or external events. Liberal and conservative, ethnic overseas Koreans and westerners, the Russians and the Japanese — they all pretty much agree that such change is desirable. Between now and then, however, North Korea's leadership must be dealt with. The argument is how. Should we ignore Kim Jong-il, engage with him, or push for his collapse?

As much as we may wish that the regime could be surgically removed, if for no other reason than to free the North Korean people from its controls, internal issues of governance alone rarely move other countries to such action. Governments tend to act out of national self-interest, not altruism.

With his development of nuclear weapons, Kim Jong-il has indeed threatened the security interests of several nations. The United States, South Korea, Japan, China, Russia, and the EU all oppose the idea of a nuclear-armed North Korea. The question is, what to do? Shall we let North Korea become the world's ninth nuclear power? It is possible that the international community has no choice, save a very risky war? If there is another option, what is it? Should we give the Dear Leader what he wants in the form of security guarantees?

Going nuclear may seem to have been a very clever move on Kim Jong-il's part, as in some ways it is a brilliant example of the North Korean ability to play a weak hand. In the early 1990s, with the collapse of global Communism, the end appeared in sight for the Kim dynasty of North Korea. But it held on. It survived because it was isolated, because of controls on information and travel, and because of ruthless suppression of even the slightest hint of dissent, but above all because its nuclear program provided a long-term insurance policy.

When the nuclear program became an international issue in 1993, many analysts initially saw it as simply a bargaining chip and thought Pyongyang would negotiate it away for economic aid and diplomatic recognition from the United States, the one superpower that could guarantee its security. However, the North played a skillful game, gaining the upper hand through threats and brinkmanship. The US, after initially declaring it had no intention of talking to North Korea, agreed in 1994 to supply light-water reactors if Pyongyang would mothball its plutonium program. This was an unhappy arrangement. The US could not verify North Korea's compliance, but the deal was better than no deal at all.

The exposure in October 2002 of Kim Jong-il's clandestine uranium-based nuclear program may not, strictly speaking, have broken the letter of the 1994 deal — which covered a plutonium program — but it certainly broke the spirit of it. It led many analysts to agree with the argument that North Korea's real objective was not to use nukes as a bargaining chip, but that the country intended to become a nuclear power in its own right.

If this is true, it suggests that the weapons cannot be bargained away. Or that, if they could be, the North Korean regime would have an alternative insurance policy up its sleeve, such as the threat of biological weapons. This may well be the case, for it is very difficult to imagine Kim Jong-il ever having sufficient trust in any deal he may strike with the United States, South Korea, or Japan. He will always want to be able to reach into his back pocket and pull out the surprise deterrent.

Put all these elements together — anti-western regime, failed economy, famine, nuclear weapons; and then consider the consequences of inaction — possible nuclear escalation in East Asia, sale of nuclear weapons and other materials to terrorists, the actual use of nuclear weapons, accidents; and it becomes clear that international consensus must be reached on a way to deal with North Korea. The longer this standoff remains unresolved, the more likely it will lurch into warfare.

Washington still wants to avoid war. Analysis by US Forces Korea in 1994 concluded that any major conflict could kill a million people, including up to 100,00 Americans. However, we should not rule out this option. Despite its insistence on taking a peaceful approach to the North Korea issue, the US has clearly demonstrated since September 11 that it is now willing to go to war, not just to defend itself, but as with the attack on Iraq, to pre-empt a perceived threat.

North Korea does not want war because it knows it would be very quickly finished off by superior US and South Korean military power. It says it wants a security agreement with the United States. But Washington says that, before this happens, the nukes will have to go. The US also insists that talks should be held in a multilateral forum. The key nation in such a multinational forum, aside from the United States, is China. A long-time ally of North Korea, China has concerns about the likelihood of Kim Jong-il prompting a regional nuclear arms race. Chinese pressure may have influenced North Korea to agree to the multilateral forum proposal in July 2003.

Aside from seeking to present a united international front, Washington's position also reflects its refusal to respond to what it sees as blackmail. North Korea's classic style of negotiation — look, I'm dangerous, I might even hurt myself, you'd better give me what I want — is falling on deaf ears. The US doesn't want to reward bad behavior. This response from the administration of President George W. Bush is reminiscent of the initial 1993 response from the Clinton administration. There is a deep streak in Washington's thinking that agreeing to negotiate is somehow itself a kind of reward. The personal view of George Bush hardens this position further. Bush has an almost theological take on individual world leaders and has no stomach for dealing with those he considers evil. Kim Jong-il, whom Bush has referred to as a "pygmy," is clearly in the latter camp.

"I think [the president] has come to the conclusion that Kim Jong-il is evil and loathsome and it is immoral to negotiate with him," William Perry, a former US defense secretary, told *The Washington Post* in July 2003.[1]

Rather than contemplate the give-and-take of negotiations, it appears that Bush would rather use US power to pressure North Korea. Although this offends the liberal instinct and upsets many

South Koreans, who see the US as more likely to start a war than North Korea, it has merits because it is based on a certain reality. If you have the power, and fail to use it, the other side will see your weakness and exploit it.

Washington is looking for help from its allies in squeezing North Korea's arms trade (which we should note is not illegal) and its drug trafficking and counterfeiting (which definitely are). Specifically, the idea is for Kim Jong-il's own wallet to take a hit. This is the first time such a strategy has been employed, and it would not involve formal announcement of sanctions. It is hard to disagree with this policy, but it goes against the grain of the South Korean approach. The Korean way is to acknowledge power — in this case, Kim Jong-il's — and seek to develop ties with it through whatever means possible. Hence, Seoul's preferred strategy has been to bribe this dictator in the hopes that he'll be nice to us. This somewhat explains the reluctance in Seoul to believe that North Korea is really going nuclear.

Meanwhile, the weakness in the US position is that it is too narrowly focused on the nuclear issue. If those weapons could be bargained away, it seems, the US could get back to ignoring North Korea. For the regime in Pyongyang, though, the issue is survival, for which Kim Jong-il will risk everything. Kim may interpret a US-led policy of strangling his dirty business as an initial act of war, which it is, and respond with some form of aggression, be it direct violence or the handing of lethal weaponry over to anti-American terrorist groups.

The US needs to broaden its objectives to arrive on the same page as Japan and China, which are concerned about their security in the region, and as South Korea, which is concerned about peaceful reconciliation and the long-term fate of the peninsula.

A more effective US approach would be to combine discreet interdiction of the illegal operations of Division 39 with an aggressive embrace of the broader issues. Why not offer North

Korea a non-aggression pact, a Korean War peace treaty — for which the North has been asking for years — a US embassy in Pyongyang, loans, and access to US markets? Why not fully back up the South's engagement approach and offer Kim Jong-il a vision of a secure future?

At the same time, could the US not persuade South Korea to agree to broaden negotiations to include discussion of human rights? This last point would need to be delicately and skillfully raised. It may be a fanciful dream but it is worth exploring. Of course, it would need to be presented in a way that the North Koreans could accept. For example, as a regional commitment to certain basic rights that China would go along with. Evidence of the gulag would need to be compiled in advance to pre-empt possible moves by the North to remove the evidence and massacre prisoners.

A comprehensive approach could create a workable peace. North Korea would get its security assurances. The US would get its verifiable non-proliferation agreement. All sides could focus on economics. Somehow, though, it is hard to envision such a smooth outcome being achieved as long as Kim Jong-il is in power. But then, although unstated, a comprehensive engagement approach would also lay the groundwork for the eventual regime change and the exit of Kim Jong-il — which, after all — is what we're waiting for.

The sad fact is that, until that happy day, the poor people of North Korea will continue to suffer.

Endnotes

PREFACE

1. Hendrik Hertzberg, "Axis Praxis," *New Yorker*, January 13, 2003.
2. See Chapter 10, note 9.

CHAPTER 1

1 A Chinese arts official who visited in 1996 said she was given the US$100 million figure by the North Koreans.
2 Lim Un, *The Founding of a Dynasty: An Authentic Biography of Kim Il-song*, pp. 9–10. Lim, a Soviet-Korean whose real name is Ho Chin, quotes *Kim Il-song Chunjip* Vol. 4, p. 157.
3 For even more of this, see Suh Dae-sook's *Kim Il Sung: The North Korean Leader*, pp. 314–24.
4 Jay Solomon and Hae Won Choi, "How Hyundai's Quest for Ties to North Korea Worked to Its Detriment," *Asian Wall Street Journal*, March 4, 2003, p. 1.
5 For more, see Hahm Pyong-choon, "Shamanism and the Korean World-view," in *Shamanism: The Spirit World of Korea*, ed. Chai-shin Yu and Richard Guisso, Berkeley, California: Asian Humanities Press, 1988.
6 Lim Un, p. 14.
7 Suh, p. 285.
8 *The Great Teacher of Journalists: Kim Jong Il*, p. 4.
9 According to the defector Hwang Jang-yop. See Peter Carlson, "For Kim Jong Il, 'Dear Leader' Is Role He Was Born to Play," *The Asian Wall Street Journal*, May 13, 2003.
10 I was told that this North Korean businessman was later imprisoned for his alleged corrupt dealings with South Korean conglomerates in Beijing, although I do not believe he was under suspicion at the time of this meeting with Kim Il-sung. The faux pas was trying to pass himself off as a foreigner.

CHAPTER 2

1 For Korean history, see Carter J. Eckert and Lee Ki-baik's *Korea Old and New: A History*; and, a more poetic read, James Scarth Gale's *History of the Korean People*. For the 1392–1910 period, see Martina Deuchler, *The Confucian Transformation of Korea*. For the Japanese takeover a century ago, see Peter Duus, *The Abacus and the Sword: the Japanese Penetration of Korea 1895–1910*.

2 Spelled "Gaesong" in the South.

3 For the most detail on Kim Il-sung's early story, see his five-volume autobiography, *Reminiscences: With the Century*. For a more critical view, I'd recommend Lim Un, *The Founding of a Dynasty in North Korea: An Authentic Biography of Kim Il-song*. For both detail and analysis, see Charles K. Armstrong, *The North Korean Revolution, 1945–1950*; Adrian Buzo, *The Guerilla Dynasty: Politics and Leadership in North Korea*; Sydney A. Seiler, *Kim Il-song 1941–1948: The Creation of a Legend, The Building of a Regime*; Suh Dae-sook, *Kim Il Sung: The North Korean Leader*; and Suh Dae-sook, *Korean Communism, 1945–1980*.

4 *With the Century*, Vol. 1, p. 353ff.

5 *With the Century*, Vol. 1, p. 367.

6 *With the Century*, Vol. 2, p. 108. Kim has been accused of hijacking the identity of an older independence fighter of the same name to bolster his popularity. The other man has never been identified.

7 Suh, *Kim Il Sung: The North Korean Leader*, p. 52.

8 Told to the author by Richard Underwood, a US interpreter at the time, who was told this when he stopped and asked peasants why they dived off the road into the ditches when he drove by.

9 Buzo, pp. 9–10.

10 Seiler, p. 46, citing testimony by the officer, Maj. Gen. Nikolai Lebedev, quoted in the South Korean daily, *JoongAng Ilbo* in August 1991.

11 Seiler, p. 56; Lim, pp. 25–6.

12 For details of this period, see also Cumings, *The Origins of the Korean War*.

13 Busan called itself "Pusan" until 2000.

14 Incheon was known as "Inchon" until 2000.

15 Chang Myun went and hid in a convent. Lee Kie-hong, an economic official visiting Washington at the time, said President

Kennedy's national security advisor, McGeorge Bundy, told him that if Chang had publicly called for support, the US would have stepped in. Author's interview.

16 From Suh, p. 192.

17 Author's interview with Kim Shin-jo, and Bermudez, *North Korean Special Forces*, pp. 83–5.

18 Author's interview.

19 According to Donald Gregg, former US ambassador to Seoul and head of the New York-based Korea Society, who was told of the plans on a visit to Pyongyang.

20 Kim Hyun Hee, *The Tears of My Soul*, p. 84. Kim was the captured agent.

CHAPTER 3

1 Author's interview with Kim Shin-jo.

2 Figures are from the US Secretary of Defense's "2000 Report to Congress: Military Situation on the Korean Peninsula," September 12, 2000. See defenselink.mil/news/sep2000/korea09122000.html. This chapter also draws on Bermudez, *The Armed Forces of North Korea*.

3 Reduced in March 2003 from 13 years for men and ten for women. See *The Korea Herald*, May 28, 2003.

4 Figures for 2001, from *CIA World Factbook 2002*.

5 Bermudez, op. cit., p. 12.

6 Figures from Seoul's 1999 Defense White Paper.

7 For a full read on Pyongyang's weapons of mass destruction, see Bermudez, op. cit., and Albright and O'Neill, *Solving the North Korean Nuclear Puzzle*.

8 Moody's did later downgrade, but cited only the North Korean nuclear issue.

CHAPTER 4

1 This is taken from Konstantin Pulikovskiy, *Touring Russia with Kim Chong-il* (published in Russian as "Orient Express," Moscow, 2002).

2 The highest mountain on the Korean peninsula, Paekdu is usually spelled "Baektu" in South Korea. It is also rendered "Baektu" or "Paektu." I'm keeping with "Paekdu" to maintain consistency with quoted sections from North Korean publications.

3 *The Great Teacher of Journalists: Kim Jong-il,* p. 139ff.

4 Both are in English on kimsoft.com.

5 This episode is taken from Tak Jin et al, *Great Leader Kim Jong Il,* Vol. I, p. 7ff.

6 Interview with Lee Won-sup, *Hankyoreh Shinmun,* October 1999: www.kimsoft.com/war/leemin1.htm.

7 This point is from personal email from Peter Hyun. His interview with Lee Min appeared in the South Korean monthly, *Wolgan Chosun,* February 2002.

8 Ibid, pp. 9–10.

9 Aidan Foster-Carter, "Dear Leader Kim Jong Il turns 50: Birth of a legend," *Far Eastern Economic Review,* February 12, 1991. Jo Yung-hwan in *Kim Jong-il: A Psycho-Profile* gives more circumstantial evidence, including a claim that the 1941 date was used consistently before 1982, and that it was also on a document given to an ethnic Korean in China by a North Korean official consulting him on Kim Jong-il's fortune.

10 Oh and Hassig, *North Korea through the Looking Glass,* p. 86.

11 Lee Min in interview with Peter Hyun, *Wolgan Chosun,* February 2002: www.kimsoft.com/war/leemin2.htm.

12 See "My Love and Marriage" in Vol. 23 of *With the Century:* www.kimsoft.com/war/r-23-3.htm.

13 *JoongAng Ilbo,* October 4, 1991.

14 *Wolgan Chosun* op. cit.

15 "Nurturing the Root of the Revolution," *With the Century,* Vol. 23.

16 Ko Yong-hwan, quoted by Jerrold M. Post and Laurita M. Denny in a paper, "Kim Jong-il of North Korea: A Political Psychology Profile."

17 Choe In Su, *Kim Jong Il: The People's Leader (I),* p. 51.

18 Ibid., pp. 64–5.

19 Ibid., pp. 75–5.

20 Ibid., p. 39.

21 Ibid., p. 79.

22 Ibid., pp. 85–7.
23 From version in South Korean *Daehan Maeil*, July 12, 2000, in English translation on kimsoft.com.
24 Tak et al., p. 84.
25 According to Sohn Kwang-joo, who has conducted extensive interviews with defectors and authored two books on Kim Jong-il. Author's interview.
26 Choe, pp. 277–80.

CHAPTER 5

1 Lim, pp. 48–50.
2 Lim, p. 210.
3 Suh Dae-sook, *Kim Il Sung: The North Korean Leader*, p. 193.
4 Quoted in Oh and Hassig, *North Korea through the Looking Glass*, p. 87.
5 "Nurturing the Root of the Revolution," *With the Century*, Vol. 23. Of course, it is possible that Kim exaggerates the role of Lim the historian and uses him to add intellectual credibility to the succession plan. Come to think of it, it's also possible that Kim Jong-il supervised the writing of his father's memoirs.
6 Tak et al., Vol. I, p. 123; and Suh, p. 285.
7 Tak et al., Vol. II, pp. 14–6.
8 Lee changed his name from Il-nam to Han-yong in Seoul. These accounts are in his biography, *dae-dong-gang royal family seoul jamhaeng 14 nyeon* (The Daedong River Royal Family Low Profile in Seoul for 14 Years), published in 1996.
9 Hwang Jang-yop, *na-neun yeoksa-eui jinri-reul boada* (I saw the Truth of History), p. 137.
10 Ibid., pp. 126–7.
11 Ibid., pp. 21–6.
12 Buzo, pp. 116–7.
13 Tak et al., Vol. I, p. 209.
14 At the time of writing, Sung Hae-rang lives somewhere in Europe. Her son, Lee Han-yong, fled in 1982 and her daughter, Lee Nam-ok, escaped in 1992.
15 Sung Hae-rang, *deung namu jibi* (House of Wisteria); and Lee Han-yeong, *dae-dong-gang royal family seoul jamhaeng 14 nyeon*.

See also "Secret Lives," based on an interview with Sung Hae-rang, *Time*, June 30, 2003.

16 Lee Han-yong says that Kim Il-sung learned of his grandson in 1975 and thereafter is believed to have become fond of him. However, it appears that the need to keep him secret remained.

17 From translation of interview with his cousin, Lee Nam-ok, in the Japanese publication *Bungei Shunju*: www.kimsoft.com/1997/namok.htm.

18 Cited by Jo Yung-hwan.

19 Kim's former Japanese chef, Kenji Fujimoto: *The Korea Times*, June 23, 2003.

20 According to Lee Han-yong.

21 AP Yonhap report, June 19, 1994.

22 *The Korea Times*, June 23, 2003.

23 Jo Yung-hwan, *Kim Jong-il: A Psycho-Profile*, section "Through Chinese Eyes."

CHAPTER 6

1 *Kim Jong Il on the Art of Opera*, Honolulu: University Press of the Pacific, 2001, p. 7.

2 Ibid, p. 28.

3 *Kim Jong Il On the Art of the Cinema*, Pyongyang: Foreign Languages Publishing House, 1989, p. 303.

4 Ibid., p. 269.

5 Ibid., p. 249.

6 Ibid., pp. 251–2.

7 Ibid., pp. 267–8.

8 Ibid., pp. 220–1.

9 Ibid., p. 169.

10 Ibid., pp. 42–3.

11 Ibid., p. 205.

12 The following account is taken from the author's March 2003 interview with Shin Sang-ok and Choi Eun-hee jointly conducted with Donald Macintyre and Kim Yooseung of *Time* magazine, and from *The Kingdom of Kim Chong-il*, a translation of a book by the couple about their experience.

13 Author's interview.

14 Kim, *The Tears of My Soul*, p. 31.

CHAPTER 7

1 See interview with Moon Myong-ja on kimsoft.com.

2 Jerrold M. Post and Laurita M. Denny, paper, "Kim Jong-Il of North Korea: A Political Psychology Profile".

3 Noted by Pulikovskiy, op. cit.

4 Hwang, op. cit., pp. 216–7.

5 This point and items below are from Lee Yeong-kook, *na-neun kim jong-il gyeong-ho-weon i-eo-da* (I was Kim Jong-il's Bodyguard).

6 James David Barber, *The Presidential Character: Predicting Performance In The White House,* New Jersey: Prentice Hall, 1992 (fourth edition: first printed in 1972).

7 See Barber pp. 9–11 for these definitions.

8 Interview with Shin and Choi. Shin said that CIA officials debriefing him were quite amused when he described Jong-il as a "micro-manager," because this apparently was the nickname they gave to the then CIA director William Casey.

9 To visiting South Korean publishers and officials. See "Kim Jong-il's Dialogue with South Korean Media Heads," August 15, 2000, website of *Chosun Ilbo.*

10 This observation from Lee Yeong-kook, *na-neun kim jong-il gyeong-ho-weon i-eo-da* (I was Kim Jong-il's Bodyguard).

11 To South Korean publishers and officials. See *Chosun Ilbo,* op. cit.

12 Krzysztif Darewicz, a Polish reporter who covered North Korea and China compared him with Deng Xiaoping in this respect. Quoted in Jo Yung-hwan, op. cit.

13 Transcript of conversation with Ho Chong-man and So Man-sul, "I Ordered them to Whine to Get Aid from Abroad," *Monthly Chosun,* January 2003, pp. 104–26.

14 From an unpublished translation obtained by the author.

15 Witnessed by his former Japanese chef, Kenji Fujimoto. See *JoongAng Daily,* June 23, 2003.

16 Sourced to Kim Jong-il's nephew, Lee Han-yong, quoted by Jo Yung-hwan, op. cit.

17 Krzysztif Darewicz quoted by Jo Yung-hwan, op. cit.

18 "Secret Lives" by Adriana S. Lee, *Time,* June 30, 2003.

19 Defector Kang Myong-do quoted by Jo Yung-hwan, op. cit.

20 Ref. articles June 23, 2003, in *JoongAng Daily*, *The Korea Times*, and *The Korea Herald*.

21 *Monthly Chosun*, January 2003, op. cit.

22 *Time*, op. cit.

23 Author's interview with defector Hong Soon-kyung, who heard of this when he was Pyongyang's ambassador to Thailand.

24 Description of Kim Jong-il is drawn from the *Time* interview with Sung Hae-rang.

25 Kim told this to Pulikovskiy during his Russian trip in 2001.

26 Interview with Shin and Choi.

27 Lee Kun-hu in "In-Depth Analysis: N. Korea's Future Seen Through Kim Jong-il's Voice," *Monthly Chosun*, February 2003, pp. 231–8. See also the same magazine, October 1995 and January 2003.

28 Quoted by reporter Kim Song-dong in "Did Kim Jong-il's Sensitivity Win Kim Dae-jung's Logic?" *Monthly Chosun*, July 2000, pp. 77–9.

29 *Chosun Ilbo*, op. cit.

30 *Bungei Shunju* interview, op. cit.

31 *Monthly Chosun*, July 2000, op. cit.

CHAPTER 8

1 See Stephane Courtois et al., *The Black Book of Communism*, Boston: Harvard University Press, 1999 (translated from French).

2 See also Chapter 12.

3 A diplomat in Pyongyang told me she had taken her child out of a North Korean-run kindergarten for foreigners for this reason.

4 Author's interview.

5 Ali Lameda and Jacques Emmanuel Sédillot. For more on their cases, see Chapter 9.

6 For Holloway's account, see his unpublished manuscript on *A Year in Pyongyang* on aidanfc.net, the website of Aidan Foster-Carter.

7 Grauhar later moved to South Korea, where he works as the director of the European Chamber of Commerce.

8 Kim Jong-il, "Abuses of Socialism are Intolerable," a discourse in *Kulloja*, the magazine of the Central Committee, March 1, 1993.

9 *Time*, June 30, 2003.

10 I'm grateful for Kwak Dae-jung for this research. See Kwak, *ookineun kim jong-il* (Laughing Kim Jong-il).

11 M. Scott Peck, *People of the Lie: The Hope for Healing Human Evil*, New York: Simon & Schuster, Inc., 1983. See p. 78.

12 Jerrold M. Post and Laurita M. Denny, paper, "Kim Jong-Il of North Korea: A Political Psychology Profile."

CHAPTER 9

1 Author's interview. Vollertsen's experiences have been published in Korean and Japanese. An English version, *Inside North Korea: Diary of a Mad Place*, is scheduled for publication by Encounter Books in October 2003.

2 See Andrei Lankov, "The Repressive System and The Political Control in North Korea," translated and expanded version from a chapter in *Severnaia Koreia: Vchera I Segodnia* (North Korea: Yesterday and Today), Moscow: Vostochnaia Literatura, 1995. http://north-korea.narod.ru/control_lankov.htm

3 Lameda's case became well-known after Amnesty International published his account in 1979. I'm grateful to Jon Halliday for the information about Sédillot.

4 The accounts related here are based on author's interview with Kang Chol-hwan and An Hyuk shortly after their escape in 1992; Kang Chol-hwan, *The Aquariums of Pyongyang*; Lee Soon-ok, *Eyes of the Tailless Animals*; and John Larkin, "Exposed — Kim's Slave Camps," *Far Eastern Economic Review*, December 12, 2002.

5 Lee, op. cit., p. 18.

6 Ibid., p. 22.

7 Ibid., p. 54.

8 Ibid., p. 56.

9 Ibid., pp. 70–1.

10 Ibid., p. 95.

11 Kang, op. cit., pp. 100–1.

12 Ibid., p. 73.

13 "The Game of Their Lives" was conceived and produced by Nicholas Bonner, a Beijing-based consultant who runs North Korea tourism trips.

14 Human Rights Watch paper, "The Invisible Exodus: North Koreans in the People's Republic of China," New York, November 2002, pp. 25–6.

15 Jo Yung-hwan, op. cit., referring to a FBIS report, November 5, 1980.

16 Kang Myong-do, *North Korean Dreams of Defection,* Seoul: JoongAng Ilbo-sa, 1995, pp. 255–72. Kang is the son of Kang Song-san, a former North Korean prime minister.

17 Kang Chol-hwan, p. 99.

18 Human Rights Watch paper, op. cit., p. 26.

19 All the camps are officially known by their number.

20 For Ahn's story, see John Larkin, "Exposed — Kim's Slave Camps," *Far Eastern Economic Review,* December 12, 2002, MSNBC report, "Former Guard: Ahn Myong Chol": www.msnbc.com/news/859865.asp?0sl=-42. See also Ahn Myong-chol, *geu-deul-ee oolgo-ida* (Those People are Crying), Seoul: Cheonji Media Publishing Co, 1995.

CHAPTER 10

1 The details of Kim the gourmet are drawn from Pulikovskiy's book and the psychological profile by Post and Denny.

2 As told by Kim to Pulikovskiy.

3 Ermanno Furlanis, "I made pizza for Kim Jong-il," *Asia Times Online,* August 4, 11 and 18, 2001.

4 Ibid., "Part 3: The great man eats."

5 *JoongAng Daily,* June 23, 2003.

6 Lee Han-yong, op. cit.

7 Natsios, *The Great North Korean Famine,* p. 24.

8 Ibid., p. 47.

9 Ibid., pp. 203–4.

10 Speaking in a meeting with foreign reporters in Seoul in June 2003.

11 Zellweger's figures: the South Korean is 125 cm tall and weighs 26 kg, while the North Korean is 105 cm and weighs 16 kg.

12 Natsios, p. 69. He quotes a South Korean Buddhist monk named Pomnyun, whose Korean Buddhist Sharing Movement has conducted the most extensive research into conditions along the China–North Korea border.

CHAPTER 11

1   Figures in this paragraph are from the Bank of (South) Korea.
2   Figures are from KOTRA in Seoul.
3   It is possible that these officials are in fact scheduled to work in Kim Jong-il's own businesses. See Chapter 12, note 6.
4   Sources for this section on economic zones: for Rajin–Sonbong, promotional material plus news reports; for Keumgang, author's meetings with players involved as a business consultant; for Sinuiju, news reports; for Kaesong, news reports and meetings with Hyundai officials.
5   For a list of investors, see www.kotra.or.kr/main/trade/nk/ nation/invest_over19.jsp
6   Yang was convicted in July 2003 of fraud and bribery and given 18 years plus a 2.3 million yuan (US$278,000) fine.
7   This point startled outsiders, but it should be noted that China's zone at Shenzen was similarly controlled — as indeed is Hong Kong — to prevent people pouring in for the jobs.
8   Gaeseong, in South Korean spelling.

CHAPTER 12

1   Told to Jo Yung-hwan by Kapitsa.
2   According to defector Ko Young-hwan, a former North Korean diplomat. Quoted by Jo Yung-hwan.
3   Figure reported by Hwang Jang-yop after his defection to South Korea in 1997.
4   This and other details of Division 39 come from Jay Solomon and Hae Won Choi, "Shadowy Business Arm Helps Regime Keep Grip On Power in Pyongyang," *The Asian Wall Street Journal*, July 14, 2003; and Anthony Spaeth, "Kim's Rackets," *Time*, June 9, 2003. *Time* translates the unit's title as "Bureau 39."

5 Author's interview with senior Daesong Bank official in early 1990s.
6 See Chapter 11, note 3.
7 *Time*, op. cit.
8 Pulikovskiy, op. cit.
9 Ibid.
10 Ibid.

CHAPTER 13

1 Thomas E. Ricks and Glenn Kessler, "US, N. Korea Drifting Towards War, Perry Warns," *The Washington Post*, July 15, 2003.

Selected Bibliography

Ahn Myong-chol, *geu-deul-ee oolgo-ida* (Those People are Crying), Seoul: Cheonji Media Publishing Co., 1995.

David Albright and Kevin O'Neill (editors), *Solving the North Korean Nuclear Puzzle*, Washington, DC: The Institute for Science and International Security, 2000.

Charles K. Armstrong, *The North Korean Revolution, 1945–1950*, Ithaca, NY: Cornell University Press, 2003.

Joseph S. Bermudez Jr., *North Korean Special Forces*, Annapolis, MD: Naval Institute Press, 1998.

———— *The Armed Forces of North Korea*, New York: I.B. Tauris, 2001.

Adrian Buzo, *The Guerilla Dynasty: Politics and Leadership in North Korea*, Sydney: Allen & Unwin, 1999.

Choe In-su, *Kim Jong Il: The People's Leader (I)*, Pyongyang: Foreign Languages Publishing House, 1983.

Bruce Cumings, *The Origins of the Korean War: Liberation and the Emergence of Separate Regimes, 1945–47*, New Jersey: Princeton University Press, 1981.

———— *Korea's Place in the Sun: A Modern History*, New York: W.W. Norton & Company, 1997.

Martina Deuchler, *The Confucian Transformation of Korea*, Cambridge, Mass.: Harvard University Press, 1992.

Chuck Downs, *Over the Line: North Korea's Negotiating Strategy*, Washington, DC: The AEI Press, 1999.

Peter Duus, *The Abacus and the Sword: The Japanese Penetration of Korea 1895–1910*, Berkeley: University of California Press, 1995.

Nicholas Eberstadt, *The End of North Korea*, Washington, DC: The AEI Press, 1999.

Carter J. Eckert and Lee Ki-baik, et al., *Korea Old and New: A History*, Seoul: Ilchokak Publishers, 1990.

James A. Foley, *Korea's Divided Families: Fifty Years of Separation*, London: RoutledgeCurzon, 2003.

Selig S. Harrison, *Korea Endgame: A Strategy for Reunification and U.S. Disengagement*, Princeton University Press, 2002.

Andrew Holloway, "A Year in Pyongyang", unpublished manuscript posted on aidanfc.net, the website of North Korea watcher Aidan Foster-Carter.

Helen-Louise Hunter, *Kim Il-song's North Korea*, Westport, CT: Praeger Publishers, 1999.

Hwang Jang-yop, *na-neun yeoksa-eui jinri-reul boada* (I saw the Truth of History), Seoul: Haneul, 1999.

Jo Yung-hwan, *mae-woo teukpyeolhan inmul, kim jong il* (Kim Jong-il: A Psycho-profile), Seoul: Chishikgongjakso, 1996, (translation).

Kang Chol-hwan and Pierre Rigoulot, *The Aquariums of Pyongyang: Ten Years in the North Korean Gulag*, New York City: Basic Books, 2002 (translated from French).

Kim Chang-ha, *The Immortal Juche Idea*, Pyongyang: Foreign Languages Publishing House, 1984.

Kim Hyun Hee, *The Tears of My Soul*, New York: William Morrow and Company, Inc., 1993.

Kim Il Sung, *Reminiscences: With the Century*, Vols. 1–5, Pyongyang: Foreign Languages Publishing House, 1992–94.

Kim Jong Il, *Kim Jong Il On the Art of the Cinema*, Pyongyang: Foreign Languages Publishing House, 1989.

———— *Kim Jong Il on the Art of Opera*, Honolulu: University Press of the Pacific, 1990 (reprinted 2001).

———— *Giving Priority to Ideological Work is Essential for Accomplishing Socialism*, Pyongyang: Foreign Languages Publishing House, 1995.

Kwak Dae-jung and Shin Ju-hyun, *ookineun kim jong-il* (Laughing Kim Jong-il), Seoul: Sidaejungsin, 2002.

Lee Han-yong, *dae-dong-gang royal family seoul jamhaeng 14 nyeon* (The Daedong River Royal Family Low Profile in Seoul for 14 Years), Seoul: Dong-A Ilbo, 1996.

Lee Yeong-kook, *na-neun kim jong-il gyeong-ho-weon i-eo-da* (I was Kim Jong-il's Bodyguard), Seoul: Sidaejungsin, 2002.

Soon Ok Li, *Eyes of the Tailless Animals: Prison Memoirs of a North Korean Woman*, Bartlesville, OK: Living Sacrifice Book Company, 1999.

Lim Un, *The Founding of a Dynasty in North Korea: An Authentic Biography of Kim Il-song*, Tokyo: Jiyu-sha, 1982, (translated from Japanese).

Andrew S. Natsios, *The Great North Korean Famines: Famine, Politics and Foreign Policy*, Washington, DC: United States Institute for Peace, 2001.

Marcus Noland, *Avoiding the Apocalypse: The Future of the Two Koreas*, Washington, DC: Institute for International Economics, 2000.

Don Oberdorfer, *The Two Koreas: A Contemporary History*, Basic Books, 1997.

Kongdan Oh and Ralph C. Hassig, *North Korea through the Looking Glass*, Washington, DC: Brookings Institution Press, 2000.

Konstantin Pulikovskiy, *Vostochnyi (Orient) Express* (Touring Russia with Kim Chong-il), Moscow, 2002 (translated from Russian).

Richard Rutt, *James Scarth Gale and his History of the Korean People*, Seoul: Royal Asiatic Society, 1972.

Sydney A. Seiler, *Kim Il-song 1941–1948: The Creation of a Legend, The Building of a Regime*, New York: University Press of America, 1994.

Shin Sang-ok, *kim jong-il e-ge bo-nae-neun pyeon-ji* (Letter to Kim Jong-il), Seoul: Haengrim Chulpan, 1995.

Leon Sigal, *Disarming Strangers: Nuclear Diplomacy with North Korea*, Princeton, NJ: Princeton University Press, 1998.

Scott Snyder, *Negotiating on the Edge: North Korean Negotiating Behavior*, Washington, DC: United States Institute of Peace Press, 1999.

Society for Northeast Asian Peace Studies, *The Kim Dae-Jung Government, The Sunshine Policy*, Seoul: Millennium Books, 1999.

Suh Dae-sook, *Korean Communism, 1945–1980*, Honolulu, University of Hawaii Press, 1981.

———— *Kim Il Sung: The North Korean Leader*, New York: Columbia University Press, 1988.

Sung Hae-rang, *deung namu jib* (House of Wisteria), Seoul: Jishiknara, 2000.

Tak Jin, Kim Gang-il and Pak Hong-je, *Great Leader Kim Jong Il* (2 volumes), Tokyo: Sorinsha, 1985–86.

US Government, *21ˢᵗ Century Complete Guide to North Korea and the Regime of Kim Jong-il*, CD in Core Federal Information Series, 2003.

Yi Sun-kyung, *Inside the Hermit Kingdom: A Memoir*, Toronto: Key Porter Books, 1997.

Anon., *Kim Jong Il: Short Biography*, Pyongyang: Foreign Languages Publishing House, 2001.

Anon., *The Great Teacher of Journalists: Kim Jong Il*, Amsterdam: Fredonia Books, 2002 (reprinted from 1983 Pyongyang edition).

Index